An Awe-Inspiring Journey

THE SECRET DOORWAY
Beyond Imagination

PAUL HUTCHINS

Imagination
Publishing

IMAGINATION PUBLISHING
Cape Coral, Florida

This publication is designed to provide general information about the subject matter. It is sold with the understanding that the publisher and author are not scientists and that any information pertaining to the subject matter was gathered through research from various websites and astronomy publications and is deemed to be accurate but not guaranteed to be so in all instances.

This book is intended to highlight the wonderful space images that are daily pouring in from space telescopes orbiting high above the Earth, as a testament to the Superior Imagination that surely went into the design of all these heavenly bodies. Any references or comments to the Scriptural quote contained herein is for the purpose of drawing a parallel between man's exploration of space and a Scriptural passage written thousands of years ago, and are the expressed views of the author only, and are not meant to convey or express any particular religious belief.

Hutchins, Paul, 1954-
    The secret doorway : beyond imagination / Paul Hutchins. — Cape Coral, Fla. : Imagination Publishing, c2009.

        p. ; cm.
        ISBN: 978-09817123-3-8 (cloth); 978-0-9817123-4-5 (pbk.)
        At head of title: An awe-inspiring journey.
        Includes index.

        1. Creation. 2. Cosmology. 3. Imagination—Religious aspects—Christianity. 4. Astronomy—Religious aspects—Christianity. 5. God (Christianity)—Proof, Cosmological. I. Title.

BL253 .H88 2009   2008937839
231.7/652—dc22   0811

For more information or to obtain a free cosmic screen saver go to:
http://www.TheSecretDoorway.com

Printed in the United States of America

CONTENTS

ACT V: A GRAND ARCHITECT REVEALED AND COMPLETED
A Special Star is Born

THE GALLERY OF A FORMALLY UNKNOWN
Artist With Imagination Supreme

INTRODUCTION

THIS BOOK IS ABOUT IMAGINATION AND THE INTRIGUING ROLE IMAG-INATION plays in creating all things new. This book explores the question: If man's imagination is responsible for everything devised and created by man, then whose imagination is responsible for the incredible universe represented by these amazing photos? This is not intended to be a detailed book on astronomy, although it touches on it to give you some background on the inspiring space photos contained herein. It is not intended to be a book on religion, even though it calls your attention to a very curious and profound passage from the scriptures in the Book of Isaiah written 2,700 years ago.

It is, however, intended to show you, through this incredible photo gallery and findings from space what is now coming to light about the universe as never before, and give you reason to pause and ponder these questions: Could a Supreme Imagination be responsible for all of these things? Could it be the same One who has extended us the following invitation: "Look up into the heavens. Who created all the stars?"

Of all the generations that have ever lived, we alone, through imagination, have developed the technology to respond to this invitation. We have stumbled upon a Secret Doorway through which we can now see the universe in a way that no other humans ever have. A Grand Drama on a universal scale is playing out before our eyes. Other questions to ponder are: Have we been led to this point in history and given this technology by the One responsible for all these things? Are we, unbeknownst to ourselves, merely responding to His invitation to look at His works and to acknowledge His power—a power that is beyond our comprehension?

When you look at this collection of heavenly bodies and study the findings, it becomes obvious that the One responsible has an imagination far superior to that of mere mortals. Upon investigation, it becomes stunningly clear that the dynamic power and energy behind these cosmic wonders are incomprehensible to the human mind.

In reviewing these findings from space it is humbling to realize how inconsequential we are in comparison to the size of the rest of the universe. We have been blessed with a wonderful and curious gift called imagination, and we have used it to envision the future, design and create things that bring us joy, and explore this wondrous planet. Now, as a result of our imagination, we have technology that has opened up a once Secret Doorway to the heavens to explore the endless universe. This technology can expand our knowledge and deepen our appreciation of the Superior Imagination that surely went into the design of these galactic works of art.

From pyramids to flying telescopes, what man has conceived and brought about through the use of imagination pales in comparison to what is beyond this Secret Doorway. The Grand Drama played out on the following pages presents the works of a Grand Architect and Artist without peer, who surely, through the use of His Supreme Imagination, has brought about these heavenly works, which number in the billions. These are living works of art, powered by dynamic energy, as if they moved about in the most ambitious symphony, conducted by a Grand Musical Conductor.

PROLOGUE

"To whom will you compare me? Who is my equal?" asks the Holy One. Look up into the heavens. Who created all the stars? He brings them out like an army, one after another, calling each by its name. Because of his great power and incomparable strength, not a single one is missing.

When the ancient prophet Isaiah transcribed those words, he could not have imagined the elevated meaning they would acquire as a result of man's expanded imagination later on in history.

On the following pages is a real-life drama being played out like a silent motion picture—one frame at a time. Each frame tells its own awe-inspiring story; yet, collectively, they recite the Grandest Story ever told: the Creation of the Universe in detail never before revealed.

What I present to you in this book is merely what I perceive, through my own imagination, as to how this Grand Drama came into view through man's use of imagination, starting with the invention of the telescope. Also, I am demonstrating how imagination plays an intriguing role in the creation of all things, including our incredible universe. You and I find ourselves at the center of this story, as if we had a front row seat in front of a super-IMAX screen, taking in all the drama being presented.

As we each enter the theater and take our seats, we have a choice to make. Either we believe that the unfolding drama is being brought to us by a Superior Architect with Imagination Supreme, with power and dynamic energy far beyond our comprehension, or

decide it came about randomly on its own, devoid of intelligent design and Supreme Imagination. Regardless of your choice, the invitation to behold wonderful things no human eyes have never seen has been graciously extended too each of us.

To understand how this drama came to be and is now being played out, we first need to look at this curious thing we call imagination and what role it has played to bring this drama into view for the entire world to see. We must come to understand how the use of Supreme Imagination can be the only explanation for the Grandest Drama ever beheld by human eyes.

I invite you to sit back and enjoy an awe-inspiring view as you explore the incredible universe, expand your imagination, and ponder the limitless possibilities for our future as you respond to that ancient invitation to: *"Look up into the heavens. Who created all the stars?"*

Who conceived this curious thing; we call Imagination?

ACT I

IMAGINATION

THE DRIVING FORCE BEHIND ALL CREATIVE WORKS

"Imagination is everything. It is the preview of life's coming attractions." Albert Einstein (1879-1955)

All things created, from the smallest to the largest, are first conceived in the mind and then driven by the force of imagination to make them real. Everything achieved by man and considered great by many was driven by Imagination—the dynamic force that shapes our world.

Imagination is the force that drove the artist to first create in his mind and then bring to reality works of art like the *Mona Lisa* (Leonardo da Vinci) and *Water Lilies* (Claude Monet).

It is the driving force that impelled the architect to first create in his mind and then bring to reality great works like the Great Pyramid of Cheops (Egyptian Pharaoh Khufu of the Fourth Dynasty) and the Eiffel Tower (Alexandre Gustave Eiffel).

It is the force that drove the inventor to first conceive in his mind and then bring to reality the dream of human flight (Brothers Orville and Wilbur Wright) and the phonograph (Thomas Edison).

It is the force that drove the musician to first compose in his mind and then bring to life—*The Brandenburg Concertos* (Johann Sebastian Bach) and *Pastoral* (Ludwig van Beethoven).

It is the force that drove the scientist to discover the law of gravity—(Isaac Newton) and the Law of Relativity (Albert Einstein).

It is the force that drove the writer/poet to first create in his mind and then bring to life—*Romeo and Juliet* and *Hamlet* (William Shakespeare) and "I'm Nobody! Who are you?" (Emily Dickinson).

These works, along with all others, were inspired by creative imagination and, in one way or another, have shaped our world. The entire life experience of man has revealed that nothing we have designed, invented, conceived, or brought into existence, came about void of imagination. This fact brings us to this very important question: If man's imagination is the driving force that shapes our world, then whose imagination is the driving force that shaped the universe?

***When you imagine big,
what you imagine will take on a life of its own.***

ACT II

IMAGINATION

The Driving Force That Shapes Our World

Imagination
The Driving Force That Shapes Our World

A world without imagination would be no world at all, sad to say. In fact, our world would be a dull and boring place if it were not for this intriguing gift we all possess.

Imagination shapes our world. From the artist to the inventor, each is driven by a small inner voice that inspires them to do the impossible, the unheard of. They are driven to reach beyond their limits to discover and devise all things new. Imagination has given us variety, excitement, and the anticipation of what may materialize in the future.

From the earliest days of our existence, humans have taken raw materials from the Earth and, through imagination, formed and shaped them from basic materials into useful devices, just as a potter or sculptor takes a lump of clay and, through his or her imagination, creates something beautiful and useful.

In the beginning, man ground stones and shaped them into tools. In time, he learned how to melt copper and steel ore and to forge them into axes for cutting trees and tools to cultivate the ground. These advances provided shelter, simple houses, and food.

With each passing generation, more raw materials were taken from the earth and turned into many useful devices. Through the imagination of following generations, those devices were improved upon and eventually replaced. With each generation, the human imagination grew stronger and became more creative.

Every year, we see thousands of new products and ideas brought into the marketplace by highly imaginative men and women. It is more and more difficult to keep up with all the new things coming at us. The same can be said about the arts, architecture, science, astronomy, literature, film, and every other field of endeavor known to man. It seems that man has been blessed with an unlimited imagination.

If you were to compare human knowledge and imagination today to that of those who lived four thousand years ago, you would find that there is no comparison. The human mind has had the benefit of a much greater reservoir of knowledge and experience to draw upon, gathered over the millennia. Knowledge is the fuel that feeds the human imagination and inspires it to create new things.

One good example of this was the life of the Italian physicist Galileo, who lived from 1564 to 1642. Through his imagination and experimentation he improved upon the telescope. Drawing upon the knowledge of others in the same field of interest, he pointed his new telescope to the heavens and began to study the night sky in a way that no one before him ever had.

In his observations, he discovered the four largest moons of Jupiter. Also, through his studies and observations, he began to realize, like Nicolaus Copernicus and Johannes Kepler, that the Earth moved around the Sun, and not the other way around, as commonly thought. He recognized that there was a much greater body of stars than previously believed. His curiosity led to a new way of looking at the world and the universe. Nevertheless, his imagination and abilities were limited due to the paucity of scientific knowledge available at the time. He helped lay the foundation of a much greater understanding of our physical world.

Expanded Imagination

In the generations after Galileo, many improvements were made to the telescope; and in the 1920s, man's imagination began to kick into high gear. Still, most scientists considered a space telescope pure science fiction. However, some were seriously exploring the idea. Rocket pioneer Hermann Oberth, for example, speculated about orbiting telescopes in his writings, and scientist Robert Goddard began testing his newly invented liquid-fuel rockets.

As these men were pushing the technological envelope, Edwin Hubble was unveiling new heavenly horizons. Before Hubble came along, astronomers had a restricted view of the universe, believing that the only galaxy in the heavens was our Milky Way. But Hubble used the latest technology, a powerful one-hundred-inch telescope, and made some startling discoveries that changed our concept of the cosmos.

First, he observed that galaxies existed beyond the Milky Way. Then he found that those galaxies were flying away from each other, an observation that helped him determine that the universe is expanding.

It takes powerful telescopes to study the uncharted territories of the vast cosmos. But it became increasingly clear to astronomers that the Earth's atmosphere distorted starlight, which made it difficult to obtain razor-sharp views of celestial objects.

The idea of placing a telescope in space, above Earth's turbulent air, had been imagined and kicked around for several years. Scientists pondered how to transport a telescope into space. The rocket technology pioneered by Oberth and Goddard and revolutionized by the Germans during World War II became the means of transportation.

After scientists figured out the means, they focused on coming up with the money to develop and build a space telescope. The newly established National Aeronautics and Space Administration (NASA), created in 1958, and well-known

American astronomers such as Lyman Spitzer, began championing the cause, trying to convince the United States Congress that such a project was useful. In 1977, Congress finally agreed to allocate the money; but it took a decade of research, planning, and testing before NASA successfully launched its first space observatory. Two decades passed before NASA launched the Hubble telescope on April 24, 1990. This initiative has expanded our heavenly vistas far more than its namesake ever dreamed.

Like a young child trying to climb out of its crib, man is determined, now more than ever, to see what's on the outside. His curiosity and imagination are driving him to do what seemed to former generations as impossible. In his mind the railing is not too high, he will figure it out!

Imagination is proving to be man's way out, and a Secret Doorway to a world beyond imagination. The first discovery of that doorway was made when the telescope was invented and improved upon, through the use of imagination early in our history. Since Galileo, man has continued to improve upon the telescope and taken additional steps toward understanding the heavens above, as if they were calling to him. With Hubble, Spitzer, and other modern-day telescopes, it is as if we are ascending a stairway right up into the heavens. There is no doubt that imagination will continue to play a key role in the development of new ways to explore the awe-inspiring Heavenly night sky, and take further thrilling steps that will bring us closer to understanding our incredible universe.

As one looks at the photos and the body of evidence gathered since Hubble's launch, it becomes clear that we have ascended ever closer to a world that is beyond human imagination. It is as if one were climbing a long winding staircase, twisting and turning past galaxies and stars too numerous to count. There are natural phenomena too bizarre for us to fully understand as we make our way back to the beginning of the universe. Like a wide-eyed child, we can hardly wait to see what is around the corner to excite and entertain us!

As we make our way through this Secret Doorway and ascend higher for a closer look, it becomes inescapably clear that these incredible things we have wondered upon did not come about devoid of imagination. Could we, would we, deny that all the incredible things man has created and devised up till now came about randomly and devoid of imagination? The paramount question facing us as we make our way through this Secret Doorway is: Whose imagination is responsible for all this STUFF?

The invitation extended to us 2,700 years ago, to look up into the heavens and see who created all the stars, has now taken on a new dimension as a result of flying space telescopes. Consider some of the worlds that have recently been discovered and photographed beyond the circle of the Earth—out into the far reaches of the universe.

ACT III

SPACE TECHNOLOGY

Opens New Heavenly Vistas

Hubble Opens New Heavenly Vistas

Nearly 400 years ago, the Italian scientist Galileo opened a whole new world when he pointed the newly invented telescope toward the heavens. His crude telescope detected pockmarks on the moon and satellites around Jupiter, proving that the Earth was not the only special place in the cosmos. Galileo's discoveries revolutionized our view of our place in the universe.

SPACE SHUTTLE

The launch and deployment of NASA's Hubble Space Telescope, likewise, changed our understanding of the heavens. From capturing the nearby violent death of a massive star to staring far back in time to see embryonic galaxies, Hubble's many awe-inspiring moments have brought the beauty and mystery of space to homes all over the world.

HUBBLE TELESCOPE

The Earth-orbiting observatory collects and analyzes light from visible to near infrared, seeing more sharply than any previous telescope. The telescope has a much clearer view of the heavens because of its unique position above Earth's roily atmosphere, which distorts starlight, making it dance and wiggle. Its razor-sharp vision of celestial objects has turned the "hints and suspicions" of terrestrial observations into certainties, forcing theorists to rewrite broad-brush theories.

By observing 14,000 astronomical targets, Hubble has contributed significantly to astronomical research, from our solar system to the most-distant galaxies.

INVASION OF JUPITER

In the solar system, the observatory witnessed an invasion of Jupiter in 1994 as pieces of Comet Shoemaker-Levy 9 plunged into the planet's atmosphere and exploded. The telescope's sharp "eyes" provided exquisite details on the plumes of debris kicked up by the explosion as it occurred and for several days following the expansion of the impact sites. This collision is a once-in-a-millennium occurrence.

LIFE CYCLE OF STARS

Moving from planets to stars, the telescope documented in colorful detail the births and deaths of these bright celestial objects. It provided visual proof that pancake-shaped dust disks around young stars are common, suggesting that the raw materials for planet formation are in place. The orbiting telescope showed, for the first time, that jets of material rising from embryonic stars emanate from the centers of disks of dust and gas. This transforms what was previously mere theory into an observed reality.

DYING IN STYLE

Hubble delivered many stunning pictures of stellar deaths, such as the glowing shrouds surrounding Sun-like stars (called "planetary nebulae"), the mysterious rings of material around the exploding massive star called Supernova 1987A, and the twin lobes of matter billowing from Eta Carinae. Ground-based images suggested that many of these objects had simple shapes, but Hubble revealed that their shapes are more complex.

A COSMIC COLLISION

The telescope monitored Supernova 1987A, the closest exploding star in four centuries, provided (for the first time) pictures of a collision between a wave of material ejected from the doomed star and a ring of matter surrounding it. The collision has already begun to illuminate the central ring. In the next decade, astronomers expect even more material to hit the ring, illuminating the surrounding material, thereby literally throwing light on the exploding star's history.

A FEEDING FRENZY

Hubble is also providing clues to what is causing the flurry of activity in the hearts of many galaxies. These central regions are very crowded. Stars, dust, and gas compete for space. But Hubble managed to probe these dense regions, providing decisive evidence that super-massive black holes—compact "monsters" that gobble up any material that ventures near them—reside in the centers of many galaxies. These elusive "eating machines" cannot be observed directly, because nothing, not even light, escapes their dominion. The telescope provided indirect, yet compelling, evidence of their existence. Hubble's crisp images revealed a doughnut-shaped structure composed of dust and gas around a central object, presumably a black hole. The telescope also helped astronomers determine the masses of several black holes by measuring the velocities of material whirling around them.

NATURE'S "LIGHT BULBS"

Most scientists believe that black holes are the "engines" that power quasars, powerful light beacons located more than halfway across the universe. Hubble has surveyed quasars, confirming that nature's brightest "lightbulbs" reside in galaxies. The observations also revealed that many of these galaxies are merging with other galaxies. The mergers kick up a great deal of dust and gas, providing an important clue for how black holes feed and power quasars.

GALAXY BUILDING BLOCKS

Hubble also peered across space to study galaxies in an infant universe. (Probing the distant cosmos means looking back in time.) Hubble's observations indicate that the young cosmos was filled with much smaller and more irregularly shaped galaxies than those astronomers see in our nearby universe. These smaller structures, composed of gas and young stars, may be the building blocks from which the more familiar spiral and elliptical galaxies formed, possibly through processes such as multiple galaxy collisions. The Hubble observations also show that the early universe more vigorously manufactured stars than it does today.

AN EXPANDING UNIVERSE

The universe does not remain still; it is expanding. Astronomer Edwin Hubble made that observation in the 1920s. Since then, astronomers have debated how fast it is expanding, a value called the "Hubble constant." In May 1999, a team of astronomers announced they had obtained a value for the Hubble constant, an essential ingredient needed to determine the age, size, and fate of the universe. They did it by measuring the distances to eighteen galaxies, some as far as sixty-five million light-years from Earth. By obtaining a value for the Hubble constant, the team then determined that the universe is twelve to fourteen billion years old.

A SPEEDY UNIVERSE

One of the most dramatic astronomical discoveries of this century came in 1998, when two independent teams, using Hubble and other telescopes, found strong evidence that the cosmic expansion is accelerating. The orbiting observatory's major contribution was the accurate measurement of the luminosities of some of the most distant exploding stars, called "supernovae."

COSMIC EXPLOSIONS

Hubble teamed up with a fleet of X-ray, gamma-ray, and visible-light observatories in a quest to analyze the sources of gamma-ray bursts. Gamma-ray bursts may represent the most powerful explosions in the universe since the Big Bang. Before 1997, astronomers were stumped: although they had observed more than 2,000 "bursts," they could not determine whether these fireballs occurred in our galaxy or at remote distances. Hubble images showed unambiguously that the bursts actually reside in far-flung galaxies rife with star formation.

This is an article from Hubblesite.org Titled "Hubble Opens New Heavenly Vistas." http://hubblesite.org/hubble_discoveries/10th/telescope_.and._science/science/overview.shtml

Man's Quest to Know and Understand Takes On New Dimensions

For millennia, curiosity has driven man to explore the world around him. This is how humans grow and progress as a society. Through the study of plant life on Earth, man has come to realize the importance of photosynthesis and how it is arguably the most important biological process on Earth. Through his studies, man has come to realize that marine life represents a vast resource, providing food, medicine, and raw materials. He now knows that marine organisms contribute significantly to the oxygen cycle and are involved in the regulation of the Earth's climate. He also understands the need to maintain a proper balance.

Through the study of birds and animals, many of man's inventions have come into existence. Biomimicry, or looking to nature for design inspiration, is not new; its guiding principles have served to inspire architectural works, aviation breakthroughs, designs in robotics, and a host of other inventions.

Now, with the invention of flying telescopes placed in orbit above the Earth's atmosphere for clearer visibility, man has a new world of discovery open to him. A world unlike anything he has ever explored or studied here on Earth. This world is one that was perhaps best described in an article that appeared in *National Geographic* a few decades ago under the heading "The Incredible Universe:"

> *Far From The Land of everyday, out in the distant curves of the universe lie strange and fantastic realms, unlike anything in our wildest dreams. Hidden by the barriers of time and space, they have lived forever beyond the reach of man, unknown and unexplored. But now, just now the cosmic barriers have begun to lift a little. Man has had his first glimpses of these once-secret domains, and their bizarre ways have left him stunned. They challenge his very notion of matter and energy. With Alice in Wonderland, he says, "One can't believe impossible things". And impossible, indeed they seem to be.*
>
> *In those far reaches of the universe, in those bewildering worlds, are places . . . Where a teaspoon of matter weighs as much as 200 million elephants . . . Where a tiny whirling star winks on and off thirty times a second . . . Where a small mysterious object shines with the brilliance of ten trillion suns . . . Where matter and light are continually sucked up by devouring black holes, never to be seen again.*

It is as if many of the inventions man has devised over the millenniums have led us to this point of discovery as though being drawn by an invisible force much like that of a magnet. As we look out upon this world, it forces us to see that we are a small but important part of a much bigger picture. This is a world our fore-fathers knew nothing of, even though they, too, had been drawn along in the quest to know and understand why are we here and what our purpose is.

This new world is so immense, we can only measure its distance in light-years. (A light-year is the distance light travels in a year at the speed of 186,282 miles a second, which is equivalent to six trillion miles.) To put it into perspective, think of the Earth as a speck of dust, then place that speck of dust onto a grain of sand, which would represent our Sun; then place that grain of sand onto a dime, which would represent our Milky Way galaxy; and then place that dime onto the Earth, which would represent the known universe.

When we look in perspective at our place in the universe, the Earth appears to be but a speck of dust. Yet, here we are, on this planet, which to man seemed bigger than life until he discovered this Secret Doorway that has revealed a world far beyond anything he could ever have imagined. As we look upon this new world, it becomes stunningly clear that it is not of man's making. Yet, we have been privileged as pioneers to be the first to discover it through the use of our imagination. It will be up to future generations to build upon our knowledge and use their own imaginations to take additional materials from the Earth to sculpt and devise a means to travel through that Doorway to explore a strange new world unexplored up to the present.

As we peer through this Doorway to the heavens and look upon these heavenly bodies, we find ourselves awed by their grandeur. The pressing question becomes too large to ignore. **Who is responsible for all these things?** Could it be that we are now peering into the mind of a Supreme Architect with an imagination far beyond that of mere mortals? **Could we be peering into the mind of Imagination Supreme?**

ACT IV

A GRAND ARCHITECT IS REVEALED

RESULTING FROM 400 YEARS OF MAN'S IMAGINATION

Hubble in orbit, 353 miles above Earth, peering into the universe.

Gazing Into Our Universe: Peering Into the Mind of Imagination Supreme

The Hubble, as it has become known, has opened up a whole new frontier of discoveries in the heavens. It is as though we have been given a peek into the mind of Imagination Supreme. We have discovered wonderful things, yet they are so vast and complex that it is difficult for the human mind to comprehend.

According to NASA:

> *Hubble's discoveries have transformed the way scientists look at the universe. It has beamed hundreds of thousands of images back to Earth, shedding light on many of the great mysteries of astronomy. Its gaze has helped determine the age of the universe, the identity of quasars, and the existence of dark energy. Its ability to show the universe in unprecedented detail has turned astronomical conjectures into concrete certainties. It has winnowed down the collection of theories about the universe even as it sparked new ones, clarifying the path for future astronomers.*

The universe we can see with the naked eye is only a tiny fraction of the universe that exists. With the invention of telescopes, and through the use of his imagination, man has discovered a world far beyond his own comprehension. A world where time seems endless and dimension and space have no boundaries. A world where an unexplainable energy seems to be emitting from every direction, a universe so superior to conceptualizing that it staggers human imagination, a universe so vast that it makes our solar system as insignificant as a single grain of sand upon the sea shore!

When we look at the awe-inspiring photos taken by the Hubble, Spitzer, and other space telescopes, it looks as if these scenes were meticulously painted by brush onto a black-velvet canvas by a Great Artist with imagination without compare. The reality is that they are not mere paintings by mortals; but a living orchestra of heavenly bodies playing in concert, millions of light-years away, on a scale incomprehensible to the imagination of man.

With the invention of space telescopes orbiting above the Earth, man has elevated himself closer to the heavens to peer deep into space, as though he were ascending a winding staircase to reach the stars.

One has to wonder why we have been given this glimpse into Imagination Supreme. Could it be that man, unbeknownst to himself, is merely responding to that invitation given over 2,700 years ago, found written in an ancient book? Can we deny or resist this invitation?

"Look up into the heavens. Who created all the stars?"

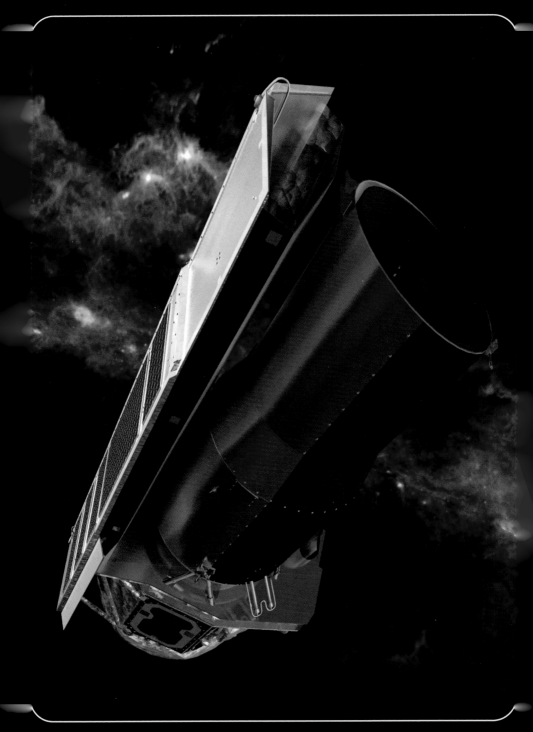

Unveiling Long-Hidden Secrets of the Universe

For millennia, man has gazed at the night sky in hopes of unveiling its secrets and revealing the mysteries about how it came about and what the meaning of it all is. Up until this generation, man's sight into the vast unknown has been limited by the Earth's atmosphere, which like a veil distorted our view of distant worlds far beyond our reach. With the successful launch of the Hubble telescope in 1990 to orbit above Earth's atmosphere and peer out into the universe without a subject-distorting veil, man achieved a major breakthrough in unveiling the secrets of those distant worlds. But, even in deep space, there are things still kept from Hubble's gaze. Many regions of space are filled with vast dense clouds of gas and dust, which block the view and remain hidden from optical telescopes.

The Spitzer, as it is called today, but formerly known as the Space Infrared Telescope Facility (SIRTF), is an infrared cousin of the Hubble Space Telescope that followed Hubble into space in 2003. To study stars, galaxies, and planetary disks, Spitzer detects infrared—longer wavelength—light that our eyes cannot see. It detects the infrared energy, or heat, radiated by objects in space and is able to detect dust disks around stars. This is considered an important signpost of planetary formation.

It allows the observatory back here on Earth to see the dust and to see through it by delivering light to advanced, large-format, infrared detector arrays. Spitzer is the largest infrared telescope ever launched into space. Its highly sensitive instruments give us a unique view of the universe and allow us to peer into regions of space which are hidden from optical telescopes.

> *According to NASA, "the Spitzer mission is the fourth and final observatory under NASA's Great Observatories program, which also includes the Hubble Space Telescope, Chandra X-Ray Observatory, and Compton Gamma Ray Observatory. It is also the first new mission under NASA's Origins program, which seeks to answer the questions: "Where did we come from?" "Are we alone?"*

Once hidden secrets about the universe are slowly being revealed as man, through his imagination, advances space-telescope technology to the edge. Man has long harbored a burning desire to know where he came from, and if he is alone. This is driving the human imagination to do what—mere years ago—seemed completely unheard of, even impossible. This tells us that the impossible is, after all, possible. Is it not amazing? No other generation before us could witness such spectacular views of the universe, that we are now capable of seeing through the eyes of the Hubble, Spitzer, and other telescopes like an unfolding drama.

As you view these awe-inspiring images from above and beyond the cosmic dust, see if you can perceive the work of a Grand Architect with Imagination Supreme.

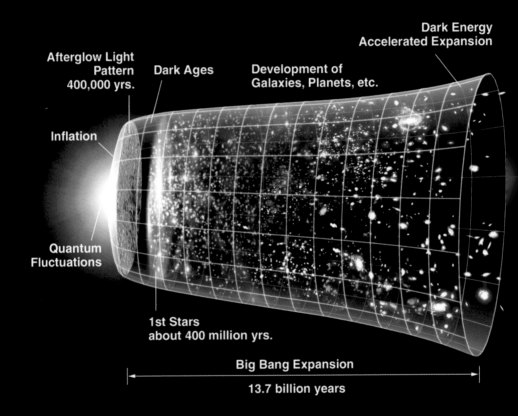

Afterglow Light
Pattern
400,000 yrs.

Dark Ages

Development of
Galaxies, Planets, etc.

Dark Energy
Accelerated Expansion

Inflation

Quantum
Fluctuations

1st Stars
about 400 million yrs.

Big Bang Expansion

13.7 billion years

Man Imagines How The Universe Began

How did our universe begin? This seminal question has been pondered by man for millennia. Do we finally have the answers, now that we can peer back into time with sophisticated space telescopes? Have we been led to this point in history by a higher power that wants to reveal this Grand Architect to us? The plot thickens!

There are no irrefutable answers to these questions yet, but what we do know is that this is the most exciting time in man's history. With newfound technology, today's astronomers are like kids on the loose at Disney World for the first time. There are so many thrilling things to see and take in that they find themselves ecstatic and in awe of it all. The stunning revelations now being made have only added fuel to man's insatiable quest for more knowledge. Already better and far more powerful telescopes, like the **Next Generation Space Telescope (NGST)** are in the pipeline to replace the Hubble when it goes out of service somewhere around 2013. See http://www.jwst.nasa.gov/firstlight.html for more details. Notice what NASA states about the James Webb space telescope under the heading **The End of the Dark Ages: First Light and Reionization:**

> *Until around 400 million years after the Big Bang, the Universe was a very dark place. There were no stars, and there were no galaxies. Scientists would like to unravel the story of exactly what happened after the Big Bang. The James Webb Space Telescope will pierce this veil of mystery and reveal the story of the formation of the first stars and galaxies in the Universe.*

The big bang theory is the latest in man's imagining how the universe began. The essential idea behind the theory is that the universe began and has expanded from a primordial, extremely hot and dense initial condition at some finite time in the past and continues to expand to this day. Will this theory pan out or will it be replaced by an even more accurate account, based on further research and investigation? Only time will tell. Remember that, based on their limited information, people in the classical era believed the Earth was flat. Through study and investigation, man later realized that it was spherical. Nevertheless, even that was not proved beyond a shadow of a doubt until much later in history. In 1959, Yuri Gagarin became the first human to view Earth from space, where he declared: *"I can see Earth in the view port of the Vzor."* He was followed by the crew of Apollo 8 in 1968. And, then, in 1972, the crew of Apollo 17 captured the famous "Blue Marble" photo of the planet Earth, and saw for a certainty that it was spherical and hanging upon nothing.

Our true understanding about how the universe began and where we are headed seems to be limited by the knowledge that we have collected from the creative imaginations of those who lived before us. This legacy is combined with our own imaginations in devising new ways to explore the universe around us to take us ever closer to the heavens. Consider this important question: *Could it be that we are overlooking the greatest source of knowledge that has ever existed, a source with a mind and Imagination beyond human comprehension?*

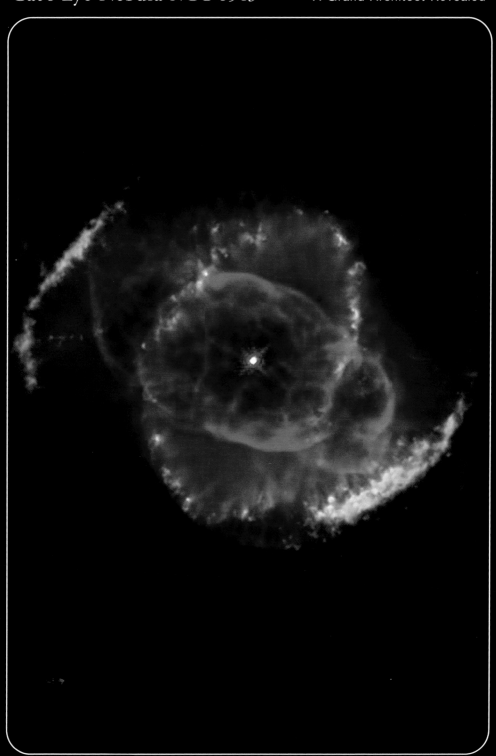

Intricate Structure in the Universe

As man explores the universe with Hubble, Spitzer, and other space telescopes, it becomes apparent that there is order in the design of the universe and evidence of a Grand Designer. But, when some look at the big bang theory, they may wonder, "How can you get orderly design out of an immense explosion of energy?" Have you ever been to a fireworks display? What did you see? You saw an explosion of energy, yet it resulted in a beautiful organized display of color and design. Fireworks (devices) take many forms to produce the four primary effects: noise, light, smoke, and floating materials.

Fireworks were originally invented by the Chinese for entertainment purposes. This was a natural extension of the Chinese invention of gunpowder. In China, they were first made by fireworks masters who were well-respected for their knowledge of the many complex techniques used to create truly dazzling fireworks displays. Yes, complex techniques required by skilled craftsmen are necessary to create the right effects, not just some gunpowder packed into a rocket and exploded. For example, pyrotechnic compounds are required to produce specific colors and effects such as the Peony, Chrysanthemum, Dahlia, Roman Candle, Palm, Horsetail, Spider, Fish, and many others.

If the beginning of the universe began with a big bang of energy, as the theory suggests, it was not a disorganized explosion like a keg of gun powder exploding on a universal scale. Hubble and Spitzer now reveal that there is order in the universe, although it appears it emanated from an explosive beginning, much like a beautiful exploding fireworks display. It appears to have been controlled and organized by technical and creative design. This is what NASA had to say about the Cat's Eye Nebula:

> *This NASA Hubble Space Telescope image shows one of the most complex planetary nebulae ever seen, NGC 6543, nicknamed the "Cat's Eye Nebula." Hubble reveals surprisingly intricate structures including concentric gas shells, jets of high-speed gas and unusual shock-induced knots of gas.*

What we are now witnessing for the first time in human history, as a result of high-powered space telescopes, is an explosive display of beautiful design that gives astronomers the same thrill they must have received when they witnessed their first fireworks display as a child. No, we don't fully understand how the universe came about any more than a child fully knows the inner workings of fireworks. When we see the images delivered to us from space and the variety of galaxies, stars, nebula, quasars, neutron stars, black holes, supernovas, and other cosmic effects, we can only imagine that these creative displays of energy were conceived and prepared by a Superior Craftsman.

It seems His intent was to impress us with a dazzling technical fireworks display on a universal scale without compare.

Small Magellanic Cloud NGC 602   A Grand Architect Revealed

IMAGINATION SUPREME

Power and Energy Beyond Our Comprehension

The ancient writings that invite us to look up into the heavens and see their splendor, confidently state that not one of them is missing. Yes, each heavenly body (numbered in the billions of *trillions*) is named and accounted for. Then, the Writer poses the question *"Who created all the stars?"* Like any great artist, the Creator of these heavenly bodies must know His own works of art, each one a masterpiece.

How can we resist the invitation to look up into the heavens when we behold cosmic displays like this? This awe-inspiring image, taken with NASA's Hubble Space Telescope, depicts bright-blue newly formed stars that are blowing a cavity in the center of a star-forming region in the Small Magellanic Cloud in the constellation Tucana, roughly 200,000 light-years from the Earth. Notice what NASA had to say about The Small Magellanic Cloud:

> *Dwarf galaxies such as the Small Magellanic Cloud, with significantly fewer stars compared to our own galaxy, are considered to be the primitive building blocks of larger galaxies. The study of star formation within this dwarf galaxy is particularly interesting to astronomers because its primitive nature means that it lacks a large percentage of the heavier elements that are forged in successive generations of stars through nuclear fusion.*

Is it not interesting that those ancient writings also state that *"He brings forth the army of them by his great power and incomparable strength?"* Yes. The Architect of such powerful and dynamic stars and galaxies in the universe would have to possess power and energy beyond human imagination. Consider the makeup of these heavenly bodies, such as our Sun, with a core temperature of twenty-seven million degrees Fahrenheit. According to the big bang theory, the compact core temperature of the universe at its conception was 1,800 trillion trillion degrees Fahrenheit, during the so-called Planck time.

While scientists often disagree on how the universe came into being, do you not find it interesting that they all agree that its source is a source of incomparable energy beyond human comprehension? Also interesting is that scientists have now discovered an unexplainable force they call **Dark Energy** that is changing our universe, forcing galaxies apart, faster and faster. For more information on dark energy, you can go to Hubble's Website at: http://hubblesite.org/hubble_discoveries/ dark_energy/

Perhaps as he peers more deeply into the vast universe, what man has just now discovered confirms what that ancient invitation suggests: *All things in the heavens and upon the earth came about by means of a Grand Architect with incomparable power, an abundance of dynamic energy, and driven by a Superior Imagination.*

V838 Monocerotis Light Echo

A Grand Architect Revealed

Blueprints to a Grand Architecture Discovered

Considering that this Grand Architecture just now coming to light was billions of years in the making, it makes one wonder what Supreme Imagination was used to conceive and create such an undertaking. We can only stand in awe when we consider The Mind behind the universe.

If man, with his creative imagination, has conceived all the things that he has developed from his beginning on this planet, including trying to shape and improve the world and the manufacture of flying telescopes to circle the Earth to peer out into the vast universe—is it such a stretch for us to imagine that our Grand Universe and our home, the Earth, and life itself, were conceived and created by someone with a Superior Imagination?

Notice what NASA had to say about the V838 Monocerotis Light Echo:

> **Starry Night,** *Vincent van Gogh's famous painting, is renowned for its bold whorls of light sweeping across a raging night sky. Although this image of the heavens came only from the artist's restless imagination, a new picture from NASA's Hubble Space Telescope bears remarkable similarities to the van Gogh work, complete with never-before-seen spirals of dust swirling across trillions of miles of interstellar space.*

> *This image, obtained with the Advanced Camera for Surveys on February 8, 2004, is Hubble's latest view of an expanding halo of light around a distant star, named V838 Monocerotis (V838 Mon). The illumination of interstellar dust comes from the red supergiant star at the middle of the image, which gave off a flashbulb-like pulse of light two years ago. V838 Mon is located about 20,000 light-years away from Earth in the direction of the constellation Monoceros, placing the star at the outer edge of our Milky Way galaxy.*

If Vincent van Gogh's imagination is responsible for the painting *Starry Night,* then what inspired him? Could it have been the mesmerizing grandeur of the night sky? Think of the imagination that went into this Heavenly Masterpiece called Monocerotis Light Echo!

It is as if Hubble and Spitzer have stumble upon the blueprints of Heaven, and Earth. New prints and discoveries, like the V838 Monocerotis Light Echo, are being uncovered every day and transmitted back to Earth to be pored over to glean every detail of this Grand Architecture. The universe is being revealed one frame at a time, as if it was recorded for us long ago as a testament to the imagination responsible for all these incredible things.

Out of the Darkness Come Stars (Artist Concept) A Grand Architect Revealed

IMAGINATION SUPREME

A Massive Cosmic Vineyard Spreads Out Into Infinity

From an early time, our universe took on a majestic appearance. Spun from an incomprehensible source of matter, light, and energy, it has grown like a massive cosmic vineyard as it spread out into infinity. With its roots firmly planted, it has budded and blossomed forth, stars without number, collecting in massive black holes to become the central powerhouse for galaxies that, in turn, have given birth to billions of other stars, that, in turn, have birthed planets and other cosmic phenomenon.

As its cosmic vines sprawled out, the universe has produced a kaleidoscope of cosmic nebula, like exploding fireworks displays, as if painted with colorful cosmic dust. These nebulas are like masterpieces of art displayed in a cosmic gallery throughout the heavens. Its billions of galaxies have formed into galaxy clusters, like grapes on a vine, with each galaxy displaying its own personality, beauty, and intrigue.

Is it not interesting that from one tiny grape seed nurtured over time, you can grow a massive vineyard that covers an entire continent with grape clusters as far as the eye can see? What a miracle of life wrapped up in such a tiny seed! Could this same miracle of the creative process shed light on how our Grand Universe formed, expanded, and spread out over billions of years like a colossal vineyard? The clusters of galaxies exist as far as man's space telescopes can see. A NASA news release (November 2, 2005) discussed our early universe:

Scientists See Light that May Be from First Objects in Universe

Scientists using NASA's Spitzer Space Telescope say they have detected light that may be from the earliest objects in the universe. If confirmed, the observation provides a glimpse of an era more than 13 billion years ago when, after the fading embers of the theorized Big Bang gave way to millions of years of pervasive darkness, the universe came alive. This artist's concept shows what the very early universe might have looked like, just after its first stars began bursting onto the scene. This light could be from the very first stars or perhaps from hot gas falling into the first black holes . . . Scientists theorize that almost instantaneously after the Big Bang, matter began clumping together due to quantum fluctuations. Gravity kicked in next, causing those clumps to grow into larger clouds of invisible hydrogen gas (colored blue here). Eventually, around 200 to 400 million years after the Big Bang, the gas ignited and stars were born.

Could the universe be feeding upon the soil of dark energy as it continues to expand outward from its small but powerful seed of origin? Perhaps we will never fully understand how the universe was formed, but isn't it wonderful that we now have discovered a Secret Doorway to the heavens to help us in our quest to know?

A Mere Reflection of the Reality

Take a good look at the Hubble Ultra Deep Field photo taken by the Hubble space telescope. This picture is an image of a tiny core sample of space, viewing as many as 10,000 or more galaxies. Notice what NASA says about the image:

Galaxies, galaxies everywhere—as far as NASA's Hubble Space Telescope can see. This view of nearly 10,000 galaxies is the deepest visible-light image of the cosmos. Called the Hubble Ultra Deep Field, this galaxy-studded view represents a "deep" core sample of the universe, cutting across billions of light-years. Peering into the Ultra Deep Field is like looking through an eight-foot-long soda straw.

Believe it or not, this single photo is the culmination of 400 years of man's imagination, determination, blood, sweat, and tears, as well as billions of dollars to capture it. Consider for a moment all that went into capturing this fuzzy yet magnificent image.

To plumb the genesis of man's romance with space, we must first go back over 400 years, to when the telescope was invented in the seventeenth century. This marked, in earnest, the start of man's desire to explore space, coincident with the study of astronomy. It would require the discovery of gravity by Sir Isaac Newton, and relativity by Albert Einstein. Next, it would require the invention of electricity, radio transmission, manned air flight, rocket propulsion, computers, digital photography, the space shuttle (considered by some to be the most complex machine ever devised by man), and the Hubble space telescope; plus millions of man hours, billions of dollars, and a host of other inventions. Then, finally, 800 separate exposures of the same spot in space.

Consider this **photo** is only a **mere image of the reality**. If it took all that human imagination, thought, study, and centuries of effort to create a single photo image of a tiny portion of the universe, then what is to be said about the imagination and effort that went into the creation of the universe itself? Like a Grand Conductor, conducting a harmonious orchestra, it appears that the Architect of the heavens intends to impress upon us the superior wisdom and power he possessed as the Grand Conductor of the universe, and to demonstrate the impossibility of man to govern the heavens.

The reality could only come from billions of years of imagination, thought, and effort on the part of One with a mind of Superior Imagination. For one to imagine that the universe came about by chance without a Superior Designer, would be like imagining that the Hubble space telescope came about on its own, without a designer. It just happened to be orbiting the earth, taking photo images of the universe without man's imagination or effort. It just happened to take 800 photos of the same spot in space in 400 orbits around earth from September 24, 2003 and January 16, 2004, to deliver such a magnificent photo. Who would be foolish enough to believe such a story? Could you convince NASA that Hubble was just a random object that just happened along without their creative genius?

Where Do Light and Darkness Come From?

When Galileo peered up at the heavens, he could only see a tiny fraction of what we now see with the aid of sophisticated telescopes. With space telescopes, man has discovered that there is much more light and darkness out there than the Sun and night sky that Galileo was able to observe with his eyes. But even the most powerful telescopes cannot see to the end of darkness as they peer out quadrillions upon quadrillions of miles into space.

Our Sun, with a core temperature of twenty-seven million degrees, has a mass of about 333,000 times the Earth's. The Sun is 1,391,000 kilometers (862,400 miles) in diameter, Earth is 12,742 kilometers (7,900 miles) in diameter, yet our Sun is only one of perhaps 400 billion other stars in our Milky Way galaxy, a tiny speck among the billions of *trillions* of other stars in the universe. Just consider the light produced by the Sombrero Galaxy. It is thought to be some 50,000 light-years across (about half the diameter of our Milky Way galaxy), yet containing some 800 billion stars. Astronomers think outer material may be falling into a compact core that suggests there may be a super-massive black hole weighing as much as a billion stars at the heart of it. Notice what NASA had to say about this galaxy:

> *NASA's Hubble Space Telescope has trained its razor-sharp eye on one of the universe's most stately and photogenic galaxies, the Sombrero galaxy, Messier 104 (M104). The galaxy's hallmark is a brilliant-white bulbous core encircled by the thick dust lanes comprising the spiral structure of the galaxy. As seen from Earth, the galaxy is tilted nearly edge-on. We view it from just six degrees north of its equatorial plane. This brilliant galaxy was named the Sombrero because of its resemblance to the broad rim and high-topped Mexican hat.*

When you consider that the Sombrero Galaxy is only one of perhaps more than one hundred billion other galaxies in the known universe, does it not cause you to ponder the question "Where does light come from?" Galileo could never have known that there was so much more to learn and behold beyond his view of the night sky and the brilliance of our distant Sun!

As we ponder the source of light and darkness, we have to stand in awe of the Imagination and dynamic power behind such incredible bodies of light. We have to wonder how much more lies beyond our present vision of the universe. How much more will future generations, with even more sophisticated equipment, be privileged to see and perhaps, one day, explore? The question "Where does light come from?" is, in and of itself, a much more complex question than we might initially conceive. Who can comprehend the answer, let alone the imagination and power that went into its creation?

Dusty Eye of the Helix Nebula NGC 7293   A Grand Architect Revealed

IMAGINATION SUPREME

A Grand Masterpiece on Display

You have heard of Picasso. You may have seen the work of Monet or the master-pieces painted by Leonardo da Vinci—but have you ever come across a master work of art like the Dusty Eye of the Helix Nebula on a galactic scale with the universe as its canvas?

The Grand Artist who created this masterpiece no doubt used His imagination, much like Picasso, Monet, and da Vinci used theirs; but instead of painting onto a cloth canvas with colored oil paints, he used gaseous layers that are heated by the hot core of a dead star, called a "white dwarf," that shine with infrared and visible colors, along with a cosmic dust storm, and emit incredible amounts of energy—as hot as 200,000 degrees Fahrenheit. He used the universe as his black backdrop, as if it were sprinkled with luminous stardust.

This Grand Work of art could not be measured against that of mere mortals, espe-cially when you consider that the gallery that has acquired this exquisite work is 700 light-years away in the constellation Aquarius and belongs to a class of objects called "planetary nebula." This piece is known by the locals as the eye of the green monster.

A press release from NASA, dated February 12, 2007, under the heading **Comets Clash at Heart of Helix Nebula,** said:

A bunch of rowdy comets are colliding and kicking up dust around a dead star, according to new observations from NASA's Spitzer Space Telescope. The dead star lies at the center of the much-photographed Helix Nebula, a shimmering cloud of gas with an eerie resemblance to a giant eye. "We were surprised to see so much dust around this star," noted one professor of the University of Arizona. "The dust must be coming from comets that survived the death of their sun." Spitzer's spectacular new view of the Helix Nebula shows colors as seen in infrared. The dusty dead star appears as a dot in the middle of the nebula, like a red pupil in a monster's green eye.

The Helix Nebula was formed when a star much like our Sun died and sloughed off its skin, or outer layers. Radiation from the dead star's hot core, called a white dwarf, heats the expelled material, causing it to fluoresce with vivid colors. This cosmic beauty, termed a planetary nebula, won't last long. In about 10,000 years, its shiny clouds will fade, leaving the white dwarf and its circling comets to cool down alone in empty space.

Could this masterpiece, trillions of miles away, just now being revealed—be the work of the hands of a Grand Artist whose imagination, energy, and power have no limits?

Exquisite Artwork From a Formally Unknown Artist

Day after day, through their discoveries, Hubble and Spitzer relay Masterful works of cosmic art, like the Eagle Nebula, back to Earth. It is as if they have stumbled upon a Grand Gallery full of never-before-seen exquisite works of art by a formerly unknown artist.

This infrared image of the Eagle Nebula stirs emotions as it silently sings in splendor of the Grand Artist responsible for its colorful hues. This masterpiece has been acquired by a gallery 7,000 light-years away in the constellation Serpens. When you look at this scene, what you see is not just a work of cosmic art but a Grand Work of creation on a celestial scale, light-years in dimension. NASA wrote this about the Eagle Nebula:

> *This majestic view taken by NASA's Spitzer Space Telescope tells an untold story of life and death in the Eagle Nebula, an industrious star-making factory located 7,000 light-years away in the Serpens constellation. The image shows the region's entire network of turbulent clouds and newborn stars in infrared light. The color green denotes cooler towers and fields of dust, including the three famous space pillars, dubbed the "Pillars of Creation," which were photographed by NASA's Hubble Space Telescope in 1995.*
>
> *But it is the color red that speaks of the drama taking place in this region. Red represents hotter dust thought to have been warmed by the explosion of a massive star about 8,000 to 9,000 years ago. Since light from the Eagle Nebula takes 7,000 years to reach us, this "supernova" explosion would have appeared as an oddly bright star in our skies about 1,000 to 2,000 years ago.*
>
> *According to astronomers' estimations, the explosion's blast wave would have spread outward and toppled the three pillars about 6,000 years ago (which means we wouldn't witness the destruction for another 1,000 years or so). The blast wave would have crumbled the mighty towers, exposing newborn stars that were buried inside, and triggering the birth of new ones.*

Like never before, amazing data pours in day and night from Spitzer, Hubble, and other spacecraft, as if the heavens were bursting with the knowledge of unknown Superior Works of art. Could this infrared image be a self-portrait of the artist Himself sitting down to work on a masterpiece? Take a good look at this image in the lower right corner. What do you see? Does it resemble a silhouette of an artist sitting down, facing his work with an outstretched right hand, as his left hand rests on his knee with his brush in hand, as if He is explaining his technique to a young apprentice? Or is it someone with a scepter in His left hand performing an act of cosmic creation?

Whoa, that's imagination. What a brilliant work of art!

A Young Apprentice in Training

Great artists will often take a young apprentice under their wings to teach him or her their skills. Could a peculiar pair of spiral galaxies near the constellation Canis Major reflect a Master Craftsman at work, training his young apprentice? Could this be an example as the young apprentice works to duplicate his Master's grand work of art on a galactic scale?

It seems as though the Grand Master takes special care to teach the young apprentice so that he will reflect the Supreme Imagination and Creative Genius that his Master Teacher possesses. Notice what NASA said about **a peculiar pair of spiral galaxies:**

> *This photo image in the direction of the constellation Canis Major, shows two spiral galaxies pass by each other like majestic ships in the night. The near-collision has been caught in images taken by NASA's Hubble Space Telescope and its Wide Field Planetary Camera 2. The larger and more massive galaxy is cataloged as NGC 2207 (on the left in the Hubble Heritage image), and the smaller one on the right is IC 2163. Strong tidal forces from NGC 2207 have distorted the shape of IC 2163, flinging out stars and gas into long streamers stretching out a hundred thousand light-years toward the right-hand edge of the image.*

> *Computer simulation calculations indicate that IC 2163 is swinging past NGC 2207 in a counterclockwise direction, having made its closest approach 40 million years ago. However, IC 2163 does not have sufficient energy to escape from the gravitational pull of NGC 2207, and is destined to be pulled back and swing past the larger galaxy again in the future. The high resolution of the Hubble telescope image reveals dust lanes in the spiral arms of NGC 2207, clearly silhouetted against IC 2163, which is in the background. Hubble also reveals a series of parallel dust filaments extending like fine brush strokes along the tidally stretched material on the right-hand side. The large concentrations of gas and dust in both galaxies may well erupt into regions of active star formation in the near future.*

> *Trapped in their mutual orbit around each other, these two galaxies will continue to distort and disrupt each other. Eventually, billions of years from now, they will merge into a single, more massive galaxy. It is believed that many present-day galaxies, including the Milky Way, were assembled from a similar process of coalescence of smaller galaxies occurring over billions of years.*

Could this pair of galaxies have been the work of a Grand Architect and his young apprentice as they worked side-by-side, creating these two Grand works of art thousands of light-years in dimension? As if performing a majestic marriage waltz, these two galaxies seem destined to unite as one.

IMAGINATION SUPREME

The Birth of a Special Galaxy

As we look back in time at the birth of the Milky Way galaxy, through the eyes of Hubble, we are compelled to give attention to it. What we see as we look back is a construction zone on a galactic scale. As with any great architectural work, the initial stage may seem confusing and disorganized to an outsider. But to the onsite project Engineer in charge, everything is going according to plan. A spectacular work of art has been crafted.

Like someone looking at a construction zone from a distance, we do not have all the details about how this Grand Architecture was constructed. A wonderful work of supreme art is indeed our home—the Milky Way galaxy. Although we can only speculate about its beginning, it might have seemed chaotic to some observers. However, we see that order grew from that. Here is what NASA said about the **Milky Way's birth:**

> *This is an artist's concept of the early formative years of our Milky Way galaxy, circa 12.7 billion years ago. That long ago, the majestic spiral arms of our galaxy had not yet formed; the sky was a sea of globular star clusters. The bright blue star cluster at center left is among hundreds of primeval globular star clusters that came together to build up the galaxy. This particular cluster survives today as the globular cluster M4 in Scorpius. Astronomers used Hubble to find the oldest burned-out stars—called white dwarfs—in the cluster. The dwarfs serve as "clocks" for calculating the cluster's age based on temperature. The cluster—chock full of young and blue-white stars in this artwork—probably started forming several hundred million years after the big bang. At right of center, the hub of the galaxy is beginning to form. Lanes of dark dust encircle a young supermassive black hole. An extragalactic jet of high-speed material beams into space from the young black hole, which is engorging itself on stars, gas and dust. A string of supernova explosions from the most massive stars in the cluster creates pink bubbles of hot gas around each star cluster.*

The act of birth is miraculous when you consider that from the moment of conception a child's complete makeup is written in its DNA blueprint. Could the same be true of the birth of a galaxy? Perhaps from the moment the Milky Way was conceived in its Creator's mind, through the use of imagination, its makeup or DNA blueprint was known, and the creative work would proceed exactly as planned.

Because Hubble's orbit is inside the Milky Way galaxy, it cannot be photographed by Hubble like our neighbor, the Andromeda galaxy. But when you look at the photos of Andromeda and other galaxies, can you imagine how beautiful the Milky Way galaxy must be from an external vantage point? Does it not make you pause and respect the wonderful works of its Designer?

Milky Way Galaxy (Artist Concept)   A Grand Architect Revealed

ANDROMEDA
GALAXY

TRIANGULUM
GALAXY

**THE LOCAL
GROUP**

MILKY WAY
GALAXY

Can A House Construct Itself?

It is no secret that every house was constructed by someone. Have you ever heard of a house that constructed itself? Of course not. Even a simple grass hut requires someone to build it. Does it not then seem logical that our home, the Earth, and the Milky Way galaxy it orbits within, would have been constructed by someone with an imagination? It is thought that the Milky Way was formed about the same time as the rest of the universe—around thirteen billion years ago. When you look at the Earth and its millions of living species, including humans, you must conclude that the Grand Architect of the universe had a very special purpose in mind when He formed the Milky Way galaxy. As far as man knows, ours is the only galaxy in the universe to be home to living creatures. Did all of this come about for our benefit by mere chance? A luck of the draw, as some would say?

As the Milky Way galaxy formed, it clustered with a local group of about three dozen other galaxies clumped in two subgroups. One formed around the Milky Way, and the other surrounded its large neighbor the Andromeda galaxy. For thousands of years, man looked up at the night sky, wondering what that white band of light across the sky was made up of. That white band came to be called the Milky Way. It took Galileo, imagination, and the invention of the telescope to discover that this white band was actually an immense group of individual stars beyond counting.

Do you suppose that it was by chance that our Sun was formed and orbits the center of the Milky Way galaxy at a distance of approximately 26,000 light-years from the galactic center? Read what Hubble observed near the center of the Galaxy. This explains why it is a good thing that we are 26,000 light-years away. In a news release from NASA, dated September 16, 1999, it reported under the heading *Hubble Spies Giant Star Clusters Near Galactic Center:*

> *Penetrating 25,000 light-years of obscuring dust and myriad stars, the Hubble telescope has provided the clearest view yet of a pair of the largest young clusters of stars inside our Milky Way Galaxy. The clusters reside less than 100 light-years from the very center of our galaxy. Having an equivalent mass greater than 10,000 stars like our Sun, the monster clusters are 10 times larger than typical young star clusters scattered throughout our Milky Way. Both clusters are destined to be ripped apart in just a few million years by gravitational tidal forces in the galaxy's core. But in the brief time they are around, they shine more brightly than any other star cluster in the galaxy.*

To be in the neighborhood of such massive stars near the galactic center would make Earth uninhabitable. There can be little doubt a Superior Intelligent Designer positioned our Sun right where it is!

Sun

A Mother and Her Children
Perform an Orchestrated Dance

With the invention of the telescope, man began to realize that the Sun was part of a much bigger universe than what could be observed by the naked eye. Much, much later, man would know for sure that the Sun was just one of billions of suns in a galaxy that would later be named the Milky Way. Early observers saw the Sun as it rose and set each day. From their earthly point of view, it appeared to run in a path across the heavens above.

Had they been observers outside of the galaxy, they would have known that the Earth runs in an orbit around the Sun to complete its circuit every 365 days, or one Earth year. Just like a mighty worrier, the Sun orbits the center of the Milky Way galaxy at a distance of approximately 26,000 light-years from the galactic center at the orbital velocity (i.e., speed) of about a few hundred kilometers per second, and completes its circuit in about 230 million years.

Our Sun is only one of perhaps 100 to 400 billion other suns in our galaxy, many of which are similar to the Sun, with their own planetary systems or planets in the making. Do you not find it amazing that our moon rotates in an orbit around the Earth, as the Earth and moon together rotate and orbit around the Sun, along with the other planets and their moons? Then, in turn, the Sun rotates and orbits with all its planets and their moons, following it like young children, spinning and dancing around the Milky Way galaxy with perfect precision as if to perform an orchestrated dance?

Year after year, the Sun and its children revolve with such mathematical precision and certainty that astronomers can accurately predict where they will be at any time in the future. So precise are the movements of the solar system that man was able to land on the moon some 384,403 kilometers away in 1969; and recently on May 25, 2008, NASA landed the Phoenix Mars Lander space probe on Mars to search for water and signs of life.

This orchestrated dance on a galactic scale demonstrates the superior power, knowledge, and wisdom the Designer of the universe has, compared to that of man.

When you look at the accompanying artist's conception of the Milky Way and realize that it is one hundred thousand light-years in diameter, only then can you begin to comprehend the imagination behind our Grand Galaxy!

Andromeda Galaxy M31

A Grand Architect Revealed

IMAGINATION SUPREME

Can You Name All The Stars?

The ancient text that invites us to *"Look up into the heavens."* and asks *"Who created all the stars?"* also states He is *"calling each by its name."* Imagine, not only does the Grand Architect of the Universe know the exact number of all the stars, but he calls each one by name. What human could come close to accurately counting all the stars, let along naming them?

The Milky Way is a "barred spiral galaxy." It consists of a bar-shaped core region surrounded by a disk of gas, dust, and stars. Within the disk region are several arm structures that spiral outward in a logarithmic spiral shape. Its galactic center harbors a compact object of very large mass, strongly suspected to be a super-massive black hole. It contains our solar system—the Sun, the Earth, and other planets. These other planets also have their moons, as well as star clusters, asteroids, nebula, and assorted cosmic phenomenon. The Milky Way is a relatively small galaxy among billions of other galaxies within the universe. It is thought to contain 100 to 400 billion or more stars, yes that is 100,000,000,000 to 400,000,000,000! Some galaxies are thought to contain a trillion or more stars. The Milky Way belongs to a local group of galaxies, comprising over thirty other galaxies, including the Great Andromeda Galaxy M31.

The diameter of our galaxy is so vast that if you could travel as fast as the speed of light (186,282 miles *a second*) it would take you 100,000 years to cross it! How many miles would you have to travel? Well, since light travels about six trillion (6,000,000,000,000) miles in a year, multiply that by 100,000 and you have the answer—Our Milky Way galaxy is about 600 quadrillion (600,000,000,000,000,000) miles in diameter.

Since the Hubble and other space telescopes are in orbit inside the Milky Way, it is not possible to photograph it like other neighboring galaxies. For this reason, it has ably photographed the sister galaxies, such as the Great Andromeda Galaxy. It is thought by some that if we could see our galaxy from a distance, it would look much like the Andromeda Galaxy.

Consider the Andromeda Galaxy's size. It is a spiral galaxy approximately two-and-a-half million light-years away in the constellation Andromeda and is thought to be 220,000 light-years in diameter, containing one trillion stars. Yes, that is 1,000,000,000,000 stars.

Are you not awestruck by the sheer number of stars in these two galaxies alone? It is incomprehensible for man to even consider naming all the stars in two galaxies, let alone in the entire universe. Is it not logical that the One who made them would be able to name each one by its own unique name? Is not His naming the stars proof that His Imagination has no limits?

As you view this image of the Majestic Andromeda Galaxy, pause for a moment and ponder what imagination and source of power is responsible for this Grand Symphony of stars, then review the words Isaiah wrote without the aid of a telescope.

Details About the Birth of a Planet

If Galileo were alive today he would be astounded at the advancements that have occurred with the telescope. The very thought of telescopes orbiting high above the Earth, photographing and studying galaxies, solar system, planets and other celestial phenomenon billions of light-years away would have amazed him. While he had a conflict with the religion of his day, he did not have a conflict with the Bible. Galileo defended *heliocentrism*, and claimed it was not contrary to Scripture passages. He took Augustine's position on Scripture: *Do not take every passage literally.* He realized the writers of the Scriptures wrote from the perspective of the terrestrial world and not from the heavens above.

When we look at the information pouring in from Hubble, Spitzer, and other telescopes, it tells us how planets are formed in darkness from dust lanes left by their parent stars. It is as if these works were recorded for us so that we can now view their incredible births. We can rewind and play back in slow motion how a planet is born, details left out in the Genesis account that Galileo struggled with. Perhaps we can now answer the question "How did we come to be?" It is now obvious that the Earth was billions of years in the making and our knowledge confirms what Galileo understood: Not all scriptural passages ought to be taken literally.

With the information from Hubble and Spitzer, it appears that light from the Sun appeared gradually upon the earth, just as the Genesis account suggests. Light would have been scarce during the many thousands of years it took for the dust lanes between the Earth and the Sun to clear away, perhaps as the planets Venus and Mercury, like vacuum cleaners, sucked up the remaining dust and debris between the Earth and the Sun's bright rays.

Each year, as man peers through this once Secret Doorway, more knowledge is unlocked about our past, especially as we probe deeper and deeper into these worlds once hidden through time and space. Until this doorway was discovered, our knowledge was basically limited to the things we studied on Earth. With this new technology, the knowledge we previously gathered on Earth will no doubt pale in comparison to the knowledge waiting for us beyond this doorway.

Think of it in these terms: if you consider that the Earth is like a speck of dust in the universe that will give you a perspective of how small we really are compared to the rest of the grand cosmos. This demonstrates how little knowledge we have discovered compared to what we are yet to discover on the other side of this incredible doorway. All the knowledge we have obtained to this point in the stream of time, has only led us to a doorway of unending knowledge beyond our ability to fully comprehend for now. Our bold quest for knowledge has only just begun!

The exciting drama unfolds one frame at a time on the following pages as Hubble and Spitzer probe deep into the intriguing darkness of space to reveal just how the planets, like the Earth, are born in dense darkness and are gradually brought into the spotlight as the dense planet-forming dust and debris are finally polished away. This drama exposes many of the details man has pondered since the beginning of time, of just how our life-sustaining planet was formed.

ACT V

A GRAND ARCHITECT
REVEALED AND COMPLETED

A SPECIAL STAR IS BORN

PAH's From A Distant Galaxy (Artist rendition) A Grand Architect Revealed

IMAGINATION SUPREME

The Miracle of Life

The question of where life started has been pondered for millenniums. Even today, evident by our unending search for the origins of life, man is still, in essence, saying, "I want the details." Little by little, the details are being revealed as a result of man's imagination through the use of space technology. Note what a July 28, 2005, NASA press release stated:

Spitzer Finds Life Components in Young Universe

NASA's Spitzer Space Telescope has found the ingredients for life all the way back to a time when the universe was a mere youngster. Using Spitzer, scientists have detected organic molecules in galaxies when our universe was one-fourth of its current age of about 14 billion years. This artist's conception symbolically represents complex organic molecules, known as polycyclic aromatic hydrocarbons, seen in the early universe. These large molecules, known as polycyclic aromatic hydrocarbons, are comprised of carbon and hydrogen. The molecules are considered to be among the building blocks of life.

These complex molecules are very common on Earth. They form any time carbon-based materials are not burned completely. They can be found in sooty exhaust from cars and airplanes, and in charcoal broiled hamburgers and burnt toast. The molecules, pervasive in galaxies like our own Milky Way, play a significant role in star and planet formation. Spitzer is the first telescope to see polycyclic aromatic hydrocarbons so early—10 billion years further back in time than seen previously.

What imagination on the part of the Grand Architect. Billions of years ago, He used the basic building blocks for life to form our planet. They would later be used by Him to create a variety of life forms, including humans, from the dust of the ground.

We may never have a complete understanding of the creative process used by this Grand Architect; but rest assured, our understanding will continue to grow with each generation, especially as we build upon our knowledge and use our own imaginations to explore the world around us.

Let us give thanks that we have been endowed with an intelligent mind and a wonderful and curious imagination to devise new ways to unlock our past and imagine our future.

Simply Dust in the Quasar Wind

According to NASA, the hit song that proclaimed "All we are is dust in the wind," may have some cosmic truth to it. New findings from NASA's Spitzer Space Telescope suggest that space dust, the same stuff that makes up living creatures and planets, was manufactured in large quantities in the winds of black holes that populated our early universe. In a news release dated October 9, 2007, under the heading: **Dust in the Quasar Wind**, NASA stated:

> *Dusty grains—including tiny specks of the minerals found in the gemstones peridot, sapphires, and rubies—can be seen blowing in the winds of a quasar, or active black hole, in this artist's concept. The quasar is at the center of a distant galaxy. Astronomers using NASA's Spitzer Space Telescope found evidence that such quasar winds might have forged these dusty particles in the very early universe. The findings are another clue in an ongoing cosmic mystery: where did all the dust in our young universe come from? Dust is crucial for efficient star formation as it allows the giant clouds where stars are born to cool quickly and collapse into new stars. Once a star has formed, dust is also needed to make planets and living creatures.*
>
> *Dust has been seen as far back as when the universe was less than a tenth of its current age, but how did it get there? Most dust in our current epoch forms in the winds of evolved stars that did not exist when the universe was young. Theorists had predicted that winds from quasars growing in the centers of distant galaxies might be a source of this dust. While the environment close to a quasar is too hot for large molecules like dust grains to survive, dust has been found in the cooler, outer regions. Astronomers now have evidence that dust is created in these outer winds. Using Spitzer's infrared spectrograph instrument, scientists found a wealth of dust grains in a quasar called PG2112+059 located at the center of a galaxy 8 billion light-years away.*

It seems that everywhere Spitzer looks it finds cosmic dust, as if there is an unlimited supply of it to be used to form new cosmic masterpieces. It appears that some of this cosmic dust was mixed with water and sculpted into a living work of art that has been placed in a Gallery known as the Milky Way—the work of art called Planet Earth. From that masterpiece, the Sculptor then formed human life out of the basic life-building elements of dust from the ground we now walk upon. Do you not find it most amazing that everything we have, through one form or another, like ourselves, was formed from this cosmic dust? The chair you are sitting on right now, this book, your house and every item in it, your food, your clothes, your car—everything is nothing more than some of this wonderful cosmic dust that was once blowing in the wind of the early universe. Imagine that!

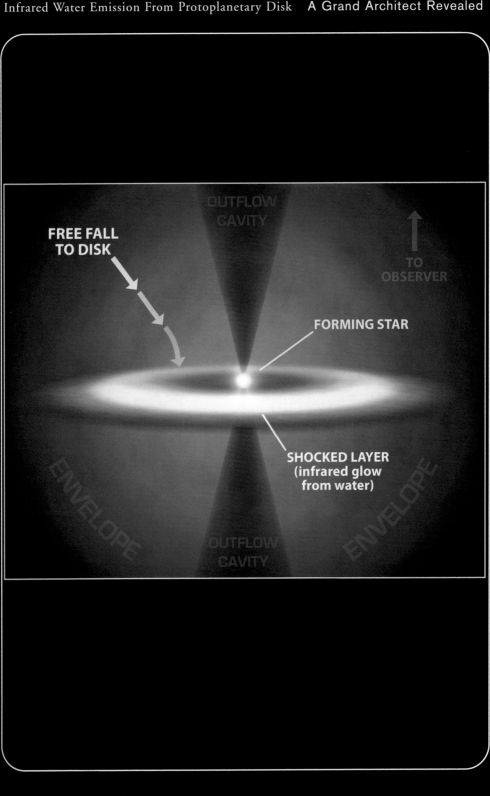

Water—The Liquid Miracle

In order for Earth to sustain future life, it will need vast quantities of water upon it. Imagine if you could look back in time and perhaps observe how water was placed upon the Earth's surface. Perhaps the scene you would witness would be much like the star and planetary birth scene now being played out in the star system called NGC 1333-IRAS 4B. In a NASA press release issued on August 29, 2007, it described a scene that could give us more insight into how water arrived upon the Earth. Under the heading **Water Vapor Seen "Raining Down" on Young Star System**, NASA reported:

> *NASA's Spitzer Space Telescope has detected enough water vapor to fill the oceans on Earth five times inside the collapsing nest of a forming star system. Astronomers say the water vapor is pouring down from the system's natal cloud and smacking into a dusty disk where planets are thought to form. The observations provide the first direct look at how water, an essential ingredient for life as we know it, begins to make its way into planets, possibly even rocky ones like our own.*

> *For the first time, we are seeing water being delivered to the region where planets will most likely form. The star system, called NGC 1333-IRAS 4B, is still growing inside a cool cocoon of gas and dust. Within this cocoon, circling around the embryonic star is a burgeoning, warm disk of planet-forming materials. The new Spitzer data indicate that ice from the stellar embryo's outer cocoon is falling toward the forming star and vaporizing as it hits the disk. "On Earth, water arrived in the form of icy asteroids and comets. Water also exists mostly as ice in the dense clouds that form stars," This diagram illustrates the earliest journeys of water in a young, forming star system. Stars are born out of icy cocoons of gas and dust. NGC 1333-IRAS 4B is located in a pretty star-forming region approximately 1,000 light-years away in the constellation Perseus.*

Can you picture a scene where, billions of years ago, the warm moist disk of materials orbiting our sun began to clump and collect together under the forces of gravity? This led to the birth of our planet. Can you imagine how it began to grow, as a young child would under its parent's watchful care? Once it was fully mature, it was then swaddled in a blanket of water and thick gloom of clouds?

The star and planet-forming events now unfolding trillions of miles away, seen through the eyes of Spitzer, appear to shed new light on how this liquid miracle may have arrived upon Earth.

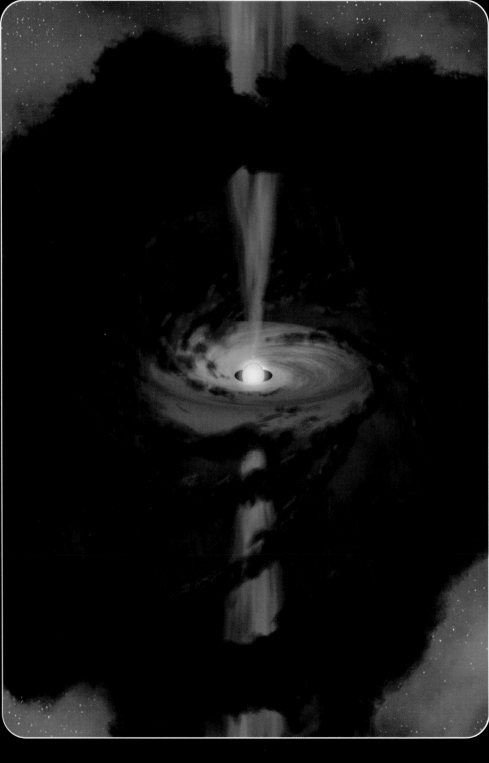

A Special Star is Born

From cosmic dust swirling for billions of years, to a brilliant shining star, the star at the center of our solar system came to life. This star amongst trillions would prove to be a special star to eventually give birth to a very special planet, our home, the Earth. If we could look back in time to see the birth of our Sun from a cloud of gases and cosmic dust, perhaps the scene we would see would be much like the one that Spitzer witnessed 600 light-years away in the constellation Cygnus in the Star system L1014, depicted in this artist's conception. An article from NASA's November 9, 2004, news release was entitled, **Spitzer Sees Ice and Warm Glows in Dark and Dusty Places**. It stated:

> *In this artist's conception, we peer through the dark dust of L1014 to witness the birth of a star. NASA's Spitzer Space Telescope has detected a faint, warm object inside the apparently starless core of a small, dense molecular cloud. If, as astronomers suspect, there is a young star deep inside the dusty core, it would have a structure similar to this illustration. Dark dust from the cloud, attracted by the gravity of the newborn star, forms a disc as it spirals inward. Often, the hidden birth of a star is heralded by bipolar outflows, jets of material moving outward from the star's poles. Although astronomers do see a faint "fan-shaped nebulosity" where they might expect the jet to be, the existence of the jet has yet to be confirmed.*
>
> *Two new results from NASA's Spitzer Space Telescope released today are helping astronomers better understand how stars form out of thick clouds of gas and dust, and how the molecules in those clouds ultimately become planets. Using Spitzer's infrared eyes, a team of astronomers of the University of Texas at Austin probed dozens of these dusty cores to gain insight into conditions that are needed for stars to form.*
>
> *In one discovery, Spitzer's infrared eyes have peered into the place where planets are born—the center of a dusty disc surrounding an infant star—and spied the icy ingredients of planets and comets. This is the first definitive detection of ices in planet-forming discs. This disc resembles closely how we imagine our own solar system looked when it was only a few hundred thousand years old. It has the right size, and the central star is small and probably stable enough to support a water-rich planetary system for billions of years into the future.*

Who could imagination that from a cloud of cosmic dust, such a beautiful life-sustaining work of Art could be sculpted? Just like a sculptor with his clay, the Grand Sculptor of the universe used just the right combination of life-sustaining materials to express His imagination on a grand scale for our benefit, when from cosmic dust He formed our Sun that gives life to this planet we call home.

The images from page 60 to 74 represent the formation of our Sun and solar system, including planet Earth, a period thought to be 4.59 billion years long.

IMAGINATION SUPREME

Star Dust Collects to Form Planets

Galileo may have wondered how the Earth was formed and what held it in place. He did not have the benefit of an infrared space telescope to give him any clues. Like a curious child, he sought answers to those questions. Only now are some of these long-hidden secrets being revealed as man looks back in time through the use of Hubble and Spitzer.

These artist concepts of the Spitzer and Hubble space telescope's discoveries of planets forming from the cosmic dust debris of newly forming stars can give us some clues. Hubble and Spitzer are uncovering secrets as to how our Sun and solar system—including Earth—were formed. Notice the progressive stages. This is how the star forms first, creating a disk of cosmic dust and debris. The planets were then formed from the dust lanes in darkness. All the dust and debris blocked the sun's light until the dust and debris eventually dissipated, finally allowing the parent sun to provide unrestricted life-sustaining light. A news release from NASA, dated August 29, 2007, about **Star System called NGC 1333-IRAS 4B**, told us:

> *In the new Spitzer study, water also serves as an important tool for studying long-sought details of the planet formation process. By analyzing what's happening to the water in NGC 1333-IRAS 4B, the astronomers are learning about its disk. For example, they calculated the disk's density (at least 10 billion hydrogen molecules per cubic centimeter or 160 billion hydrogen molecules per cubic inch); its dimensions (a radius bigger than the average distance between Earth and Pluto); and its temperature (170 Kelvin, or minus 154 degrees Fahrenheit).*

> *Water is easier to detect than other molecules, so we can use it as a probe to look at more brand-new disks and study their physics and chemistry, this will teach us a lot about how planets form. We have captured a unique phase of a young star's evolution, when the stuff of life is moving dynamically into an environment where planets could form. NGC 1333-IRAS 4B's central stellar embryo is still "feeding" off the material collapsing around it and growing in size. At this early stage, astronomers cannot tell how large the star will ultimately become.*

Galileo, Newton, and Einstein must have pondered how the Earth was formed. Through the use of their imaginations, they each made great strides in helping mankind unlock some of the mysteries as to how the Earth was founded and what holds it and our Sun in place. Man has built upon the knowledge of these and other great men. Scientists are now using their own imaginations to unlock a Secret Doorway to the heavens. Doubtless, they will make new and fantastic discoveries through the use of sophisticated space telescopes. Even though our understanding is better today, would you not agree we still have much to learn as this Grand Drama unfolds before us?

A Dusty Construction Zone

As the cosmic dust masses were brought together billions of years ago to form our solar system, along with Earth, its Designer no doubt took great delight knowing that this would serve a special purpose. Perhaps Earth's dusty construction zone looked similar to this scene discovered by Spitzer in the Ophiuchus constellation. On December 20, 2005, NASA reported in a news release that:

Partial Ingredients for DNA and Protein Found Around Star

NASA's Spitzer Space Telescope has discovered some of life's most basic ingredients in the dust swirling around a young star. The ingredients—gaseous precursors to DNA and protein—were detected in the star's terrestrial planet zone, a region where rocky planets such as Earth are thought to be born. The findings represent the first time that these gases, called acetylene and hydrogen cyanide, have been found in a terrestrial planet zone outside of our own.

This infant system might look a lot like ours did billions of years ago, before life arose on Earth, said scientists of Leiden Observatory in the Netherlands and the Dutch space research institute called SRON.

Scientists spotted the organic, or carbon-containing, gases around a star called IRS 46. The star is in the Ophiuchus (pronounced OFF-ee-YOO-kuss), or "snake carrier," constellation about 375 light-years from Earth. This constellation harbors a huge cloud of gas and dust in the process of a major stellar baby boom. Like most of the young stars here and elsewhere, IRS 46 is circled by a flat disk of spinning gas and dust that might ultimately clump together to form planets. When the astronomers probed this star's disk with Spitzer's powerful infrared spectrometer instrument, they were surprised to find the molecular "barcodes" of large amounts of acetylene and hydrogen cyanide gases, as well as carbon dioxide gas. The team observed 100 similar young stars, but only one, IRS 46, showed unambiguous signs of the organic mix.

Here on Earth, the molecules are believed to have arrived billions of years ago, possibly via comets or comet dust that rained down from the sky. Acetylene and hydrogen cyanide link up together in the presence of water to form some of the chemical units of life's most essential compounds, DNA and protein. These chemical units are several of the 20 amino acids that make up protein and one of the four chemical bases that make up DNA. Follow-up observations with the W.M. Keck Telescope atop Mauna Kea in Hawaii confirmed the Spitzer findings and suggested the presence of a wind emerging from the inner region of IRS 46's disk. This wind will blow away debris in the disk, clearing the way for the possible formation of Earth-like planets.

Is it not amazing that each of us, this Earth, and everything around us began as an oversized ball of clay, created from cosmic dust? From this clay we were sculpted into living works of art by a Grand Sculptor.

Planet Danger Zone

While imagination is the driving force behind all things new, great wisdom also was evidently used in constructing our Sun in just the right location in the galaxy. Consider a new study from NASA's Spitzer Space Telescope, as explained in a news release dated April 18, 2007:

Highway to the Danger Zone

"The further on the edge, the hotter the intensity," sings Kenny Loggins in "Danger Zone," a song made famous by the movie **Top Gun.** *The same words ring true for young, cooler stars like our sun that live in the danger zones around scorching hot stars, called O-stars. The closer a young, maverick star happens to be to a super hot O-star, the more likely its burgeoning planets will be blasted into space.*

This artist's concept illustrates the process in action. An O-star can be seen near the top right, just behind a young, cooler star and its swirling disk of planet-forming material. Disks like this one, called protoplanetary disks, are where planets are born. Gas and dust in a disk clump together into tiny balls that sweep through the material, growing in size to eventually become full-grown planets. The young star happens to lie within the "danger zone" around the O-star, which means that it is too close to the hot star to keep its disk. Radiation and winds from the O-star are boiling and blowing away the material, respectively. This process, called photoevaporation, takes anywhere from 100,000 to about 1,000,000 years. Without a disk, the young star will not be able to produce planets.

Our own sun and its suite of planets might have grown up on the edge of an O-star's danger zone before migrating to its current, spacious home. However, we know that our young sun didn't linger for too long in any hazardous territory, or our planets, and life, wouldn't be here today. NASA's Spitzer Space Telescope surveyed the danger zones around five O-stars in the Rosette nebula. It was able to determine that the zones are spheres with a radius of approximately 1.6 light-years, or 10 trillion miles.

Is it by chance or a planned design that our Sun and solar system were formed outside such cosmic danger zones? Could it be the well thought-out measurements of a Grand Architect as He laid the foundation with fine precision, based upon a scale of light-years? Great wisdom is evident in this Grand Design when we consider the fine balance needed to sustain life that is found in the design of the Earth.

A Grand Potter at Work

Like a highly skilled potter using just the right blend of clay, Earth's Designer long ago began to form the third planet from our Sun, as if it were spinning on a Grand Potter's wheel to create a very special work of art for you and me. No one really knows exactly when the foundation for Earth was laid or how long it must have taken to bring to completion. The most recent consensus from scientists suggests the Earth is approximately four-and-a-half billion years old. All great works of art require considerable amounts of time, care, and craftsmanship, and the larger the work, the greater the time required.

Imagine if you can, looking back in time. You are peering into the universe through a giant window, scrutinizing our solar system and observing the formation of our Sun and its planets. What you witness would no doubt take your breath away. You would be in awe of the magnitude and precision of it all as each planet spun in its own orbit around the Sun, each one taking on its own personality like a newborn child, sucking up cosmic dust as it grew from an infant to a full-grown planet.

Perhaps the planet-forming scene you witness would not be unlike the scene that is now being witnessed 450 light-years away in a solar system called UX Tau A. This stellar prodigy has been spotted by NASA's Spitzer Space Telescope. A news release appeared on November 28, 2007, under the heading **Youthful Star Sprouts Planets Early**.

> *Astronomers suspect this system's central Sun-like star, which is just one million years old, may already be surrounded by young planets. Scientists hope the finding will provide insight into when planets began to form in our own solar system. Such dusty disks are where planets are thought to be born. Dust grains clump together like snowballs to form larger rocks, and then the bigger rocks collide to form the cores of planets. When rocks revolve around their central star, they act like cosmic vacuum cleaners, picking up all the gas and dust in their path and creating gaps. Spitzer saw a gap in UX Tau A's disc, which in our solar system, this gap would occupy the space between Mercury and Pluto.*

Could it be that these dusty planet-forming scenes observed by Spitzer shed some light about the Earth in its early days? How, in the beginning, there was darkness upon the surface of the Earth and that no light would be visible upon it until much later? Apparently, in the beginning, the Sun's light might have been blocked, like what we see in this scene? And then the dust and cosmic debris gradually cleared away, allowing the Sun's light to appear gradually upon the Earth. Could it be that we now have some of the intriguing details to this mystery about this special planet's birth?

IMAGINATION SUPREME

Dust and Debris Cleared Away

Could this scene, of a Sun-like star called HD 107146, located eighty-eight light-years away, observed by Hubble and Spitzer, provide insight on how light eventually came to be here on Earth? Could it be that after billions of years of darkness on Earth, and in its final stages of forming, the Sun's light would now provide life-giving rays with full intensity? Following is a news release from NASA titled **Spitzer and Hubble Capture Evolving Planetary Systems:**

> *Two of NASA's Great Observatories, the Spitzer Space Telescope and the Hubble Space Telescope, have provided astronomers an unprecedented look at dusty planetary debris around stars the size of our Sun. Spitzer has discovered for the first time dusty discs around mature, Sun-like stars known to have planets. Hubble captured the most detailed image ever of a brighter disc circling a much younger Sun-like star. The findings offer snapshots of the process by which our own solar system evolved, from its dusty and chaotic beginnings to its more settled present-day state. Young stars have huge reservoirs of planet-building materials, while older ones have only left-over piles of rubble. Hubble saw the reservoirs and Spitzer, the rubble. This demonstrates how the two telescopes complement each other. The young star observed by Hubble is 50 million to 250 million years old. This is old enough to theoretically have gas planets, but young enough that rocky planets like Earth may still be forming. The six older stars studied by Spitzer average 4 billion years old, nearly the same age as the Sun. They are known to have gas planets, and rocky planets may also be present. Prior to these findings, rings of planetary debris, or "debris discs," around stars the size of the Sun had rarely been observed, because they are fainter and more difficult to see than those around more massive stars. The new Hubble image gives us the best look so far at reflected light from a disc around a star the mass of the Sun, it shows one of the possible pasts of our own solar system. Debris discs around older stars the same size and age as our Sun, including those hosting known planets, are even harder to detect. These discs are 10 to 100 times thinner than the ones around young stars. Spitzer's highly sensitive infrared detectors were able to sense their warm glow for the first time. Rocky planets arise out of large clouds of dust that envelop young stars. Dust particles collide and stick together until a planet eventually forms. Sometimes the accumulating bodies crash together and shatter. Debris from these collisions collects into giant doughnut-shaped discs, the centers of which may be carved out by orbiting planets. With time, the discs fade and a smaller, stable debris disc, like the comet-filled Kuiper Belt in our own solar system, is all that is left.*

From these discoveries it appears that young planets are born in darkness, hidden from their parent sun in dense lanes of dust in their beginning stage, until the dust debris slowly fades away and the sun's light gradually becomes visible over time as seen in this artist's conceptions of discoveries in space. This information appears to confirm what the Genesis account suggested: the Sun's light appeared upon the Earth gradually over time.

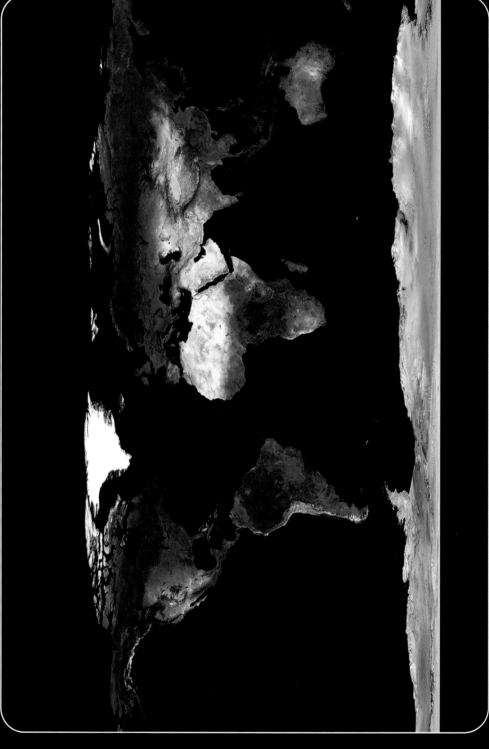

The Heartbeat of a Planet

In order to prepare Earth for living creatures, including humans, an oxygen-filled atmosphere was needed. This has been provided through imagination and the process of photosynthesis. Earth has been covered with a blanket of green vegetation of all kinds as the heartbeat of a planet.

Not only does vegetation provide needed oxygen, it supplies our every desire for food and scenic beauty. See Earth truly come alive as its heart beats in a way you have never imagined. It is highly recommended you go to this website: http://ocean color.gsfc.nasa.gov/SeaWiFS/HTML/SeaWiFS.BiosphereAnimation.html. See for yourself how the heart of the Earth appears to be beating as the seasons come and go. The Earth's vegetation expands over the planet each growing season, and then retracts in this animated display, as if the Earth's heart were pulsating and providing life to all!

This spectacular "blue marble" image is the most detailed true-color image of the entire Earth to date. Using a collection of satellite-based observations, scientists and visualizers stitched together months of observations of the land surface, oceans, sea ice, and clouds into a seamless, true-color mosaic of every square kilometer (.386 square mile) of our planet.

Much of the information contained in this image came from a single remote-sensing device—NASA's Moderate Resolution Imaging Spectroradiometer, or MODIS. Flying over 700 km above the Earth onboard the Terra satellite, MODIS provides an integrated tool for observing a variety of terrestrial, oceanic, and atmospheric features of the Earth. The land and coastal ocean portions of these images are based on surface observations collected from June through September 2001 and combined, or composited, every eight days to compensate for clouds that might block the sensor's view of the surface on any single day. Two different types of ocean data were used in these images: shallow water true color data, and global ocean color (or chlorophyll) data. Topographic shading is based on the GTOPO 30 elevation dataset compiled by the U.S. Geological Survey's EROS Data Center. MODIS observations of polar sea ice were combined with observations of Antarctica made by the National Oceanic and Atmospheric Administration's AVHRR sensor—the Advanced Very High Resolution Radiometer.

Look at the endless variety of plant life on the Earth. It, too, came from the dust of the ground. This phenomenon emanated from an Imagination far superior than that of man. As caretakers of the Earth, it is man's responsibility to make sure that an environmental balance is maintained.

Thus far, it appears we are doing a poor job of stewardship of the planet, considering the multitude of serious environmental issues facing man today. Could we not learn from the Creator of all these things how to better manage our home?

Our Little Ball of Cosmic Dust

It is a fact that an image is a mere reflection of the reality. As stated earlier, everything man has constructed, conceived, or devised has been a result of his imagination. Man's wonderful creative imagination is a **mere reflection** of the creative imagination that went into the design of the universe and a testament to the Supreme Mind responsible for it all.

One cannot look at this photo of Earth from space, as well as all the other photos captured by Hubble, Spitzer, and other telescopes in recent years, and not wonder about our beginning and our incredible place in this universe. We, *alone in the universe*, have been gifted an imagination with the likeness of a Superior Architect Who has an Imagination Supreme. Upon examining the evidence now coming forth, it becomes clear that He surely is responsible for our very existence and has given us this special Jewel in the Universe as our home to take care of.

Consider this for a moment: everything you see in this photo represents the entire existence of man. This is man's home. It was here, through Supreme Imagination, that man was formed from the ground and given the breath of life. Man, in likeness, has used his own imagination to create and conceive every invention, architectural structure, work of art, and every other material thing devised. This includes Hubble and Spitzer to capture these beautiful photos. It was all created, ironically, using the materials from the same ground that we were formed from. This Earth, in essence, is our ball of cosmic clay. We do not own the clay and we have created nothing that did not already exist here upon the Earth. We, ourselves, are merely living cosmic clay sculptures who have been permitted to take materials from the ground and sculpt them into whatever useful nonliving devices our imaginations can conceive. As male and female, we have also been allowed to carry the gift of life and transfer the seeds of life to others. But this gift is not of our own making.

As we explore the Heavens above, we are learning what these bewildering worlds beyond our home have to offer to amaze and intrigue us. At some point, will we, like Alice in Wonderland, have the opportunity to explore the far reaches of this ever-expanding universe? The prospect of exploring these strange worlds is truly exciting.

Only time will tell if man was meant to go beyond this incredible doorway into the future. Who would have thought 400 years ago that man's imagination would lead him to a Secret Doorway on the threshold of time and space to a world beyond anything he could have dreamed of? As man peers back in time with flying space telescopes, developed by use of his imagination, he has discovered that there was someone with an imagination far superior to his own Who existed long before he arrived onto the scene, who billions of years ago laid the foundations of this incredible universe we have just discovered.

Have you ever pondered this question: who conceived this curious thing we call imagination? It appears this someone has proven power, dynamic energy, and imagination beyond the comprehension of the human mind. What will we discover through our imaginations as our knowledge grows a million years from now, or billions of years from now, as we devise new ways to explore and discover the universe?

Massive Terrestrial Strike (Artist concept) A Grand Architect Revealed

IMAGINATION SUPREME

A House on Fire

As you look at this artist's conception, perhaps you imagine that one day this planet will be destroyed, either by a massive terrestrial strike like the one pictured, or by man's own foolhardiness and demise. NASA puts the planets impact risk in perspective:

> *This Artist's concept shows a catastrophic asteroid impact with the early Earth. An impact with a 500-km-diameter asteroid would effectively sterilize the planet. Scientists believe the Earth may have experienced such gigantic impacts in its youth, but fortunately today there are no projectiles this large to threaten our planet.*

A threat much greater to Earth than a massive terrestrial strike is man himself. Unfortunately, in the past two hundred years, man has done more damage to the planet and its environment than all other generations combined. When we look at what is being done to our delicate environment today, man's ability to manage the Earth is in question.

While man has been given the gift of imagination, he has not always used it in a responsible way. He has too often devised things that have brought harm to his fellow man as well as the planet. Would you not agree that this planet is a grand masterpiece worth preserving?

Suppose, as a parent, you spend many years imagining, designing, and constructing a beautiful home. And, after stocking it with food and everything that would be required to live comfortably, even some pets, you give it to your son and his wife as a gift. You ask for nothing in return except that they respect you by taking good care of their new home as their family grows. Then you go away for awhile. Upon your return, you are disturbed as you approach because you see that smoke appears to be coming out of the house. You knock on the door; but no one answers. It's as if no one cares you are there. Upon opening the door, your son and his wife are nowhere to be found. Your grandchildren are fighting and throwing things at each other, with the intent to cause bodily harm. When you ask what's going on, everyone ignores you. As you make your way through the house, you notice a black film of smoke on the walls and you find it uncomfortably warm. Your eyes are burning from smoke. There seems to be trash thrown everywhere, there are spills that have ruined the carpet, and when you look up and see a gaping hole in the roof caused by a smoldering fire, you know why the sun's hot rays are shining so brightly into the house.

As a parent and original owner, what would you do to preserve the beautiful home you had spent so much time, care, energy, and imagination on? What tough choices would you need to make in order to preserve it?

Should we not pause for a moment and think about what we are doing to this planet—our home? Are you not sad when you look up at the night sky? In many parts of the world you can barely see the stars due to all the pollution. Could man's imagination be used in a better way? Will we one day be caretakers of the rest of the universe? If so, we are off to a bumpy start!

Backplane

Optical Telescope Element (OTE)
Primary Mirror

ISIM

Sunshield

OTE Secondary
Mirror

Spacecraft Bus   Startrackers

JWST infrared-optimized space telescope, scheduled for launch in 2013.

IMAGINATION OF MAN

An Irresistible Secret Doorway

Imagine that you are eight years old and one day you discover a secret doorway in the wall of your bedroom. After much effort, you manage to peel back the wallpaper and start to pry open the door. At first you can only see through a small crack where bright light glistens. The bright colorful balls you see in the distance seem to be floating in the air. You are excited; your mind is racing as to how you could get the door open to see what awaits you on the other side.

Finally, you are able to open the door all the way. As you look out, you are stunned at what you see; it's a world beyond your imagination, a kid's dream! There are roller coasters of all kinds, swings, and planes that you can fly through the air. There are bumper cars and a train to take you all around this wonderful world you've just discovered. There are boats and merry-go-rounds. There are balloons that float, made in every color and shape. There are things you never imagined in your wildest dreams, and right in the middle of it all is a gigantic castle! Whoa, you have discovered a Secret Doorway to the Magic Kingdom—Disney World!

When Galileo turned his newly improved telescope to the night sky, he was like that young child. He had discovered a World beyond Imagination. He found a Secret Doorway that no one before him had discovered. With his discovery of the four moons of Jupiter, it was if he had cracked the door open just enough to get a glimpse of a world he had never imagined. In March 1610, Galileo published the first scientific treatise based on observations made through a telescope, known as the Starry Messenger. The question one must now ponder is this: was Galileo, unbeknownst to himself, merely responding to the invitation of the Mighty One who is responsible for this world beyond our imagination?

With the telescope, Galileo ignited a Scientific Revolution in the study of the night sky. It revealed phenomena in the heavens that Aristotle and others had not dreamed of. It had a profound influence on the controversy between the followers of the traditional beliefs of the geocentric astronomy model and the heliocentric model. The geocentric model was embraced by Aristotle, Ptolemy, and most Greek philosophers who assumed that the Sun, Moon, stars, and planets seen with the naked eye circle the Earth. The heliocentric model was embraced by Copernicus, Galileo, and Kepler, who believed that the Sun was at the center of our solar system and the planets and moon circle it.

In the generations since the seventeenth century, astronomers and scientists have managed to pry that Secret Door open a little wider with improvements to the telescope. It was not until the twentieth century that the door flung wide open with the invention of flying telescopes, like the Hubble and later the Spitzer; and soon to come, the James Webb Next Generation telescope, which will be ten to one hundred times more powerful than the Hubble.

The on-orbit assembly of the International Space Station (ISS) that began in 1998 as a research facility in space is another result of man's imagination at work to burst through this wonderful doorway.

This cooperative effort by a number of nations clearly demonstrates man's mutual desire to go beyond the entrance to the worlds beyond. Whoa! Look how far our imagination has taken us since Galileo's simple telescope! To astronomers, looking upon this unimaginable world is like viewing Disney World for the first time to a young child—it is beyond imagination!

Some key questions to ponder, in light of what we have seen through the use of our imagination, are: Have we discovered a Secret Doorway to another world that we cannot resist? Have we opened a door we can never close? Have we opened a door that we are compelled to step through by some future means? Have we found the doorway to our future? Will what we find out there give us more clues about our past? Will it make us appreciate the planet we already have? Is life here on Earth just the beginning of a never-ending adventure for humankind into the universe? Will we become caretakers for the whole universe once we prove ourselves on this planet?

What new technology will our imaginations create in the future that seems impossible today, but tomorrow's reality? Are there other Secret Doorways awaiting our discovery? Like bees spreading pollen from plant to plant to keep the miracle of life growing, will man someday go from planet to planet, galaxy to galaxy, spreading the miracle of life throughout the universe? Is it man's eternal purpose to transform the cosmos into a beautiful world, full of life as we grow and expand our imagination? Can you imagine being a part of something so Grand? Just imagine how thrilling it would be!

What children who discovered a Secret Doorway to the Magic Kingdom could resist going through it? Could they just stand there and look out in awe of it all and not be compelled to bolt right out to explore it? Could they just shut the door and forget about the wonderful and unbelievable things they saw? Would they seek their parents' knowledge about it, to see what they knew of this exciting world? Could it be that their parents put the doorway there for the children to find, and covered it up until they were responsible and old enough to go through it? Would their parents ever think of holding them back from exploring and expanding their imaginations after they were allowed to look upon these thrilling things? What do you think?

Could it be the One with Imagination Supreme, Who surely must be responsible for all this cosmic dust, has Himself revealed this Secret Doorway beyond imagination? Are we simply responding to that ancient invitation to look up into the heavens and see who created all the stars? Is this not something to ponder?

Imagination is the key. As Einstein stated, "Imagination is everything." If we could just use it only for good and not for bad, what a world this would be! Come on World; use your **Imagination—for Good!**

Imagination

The driving force that shapes our world—for good or bad.

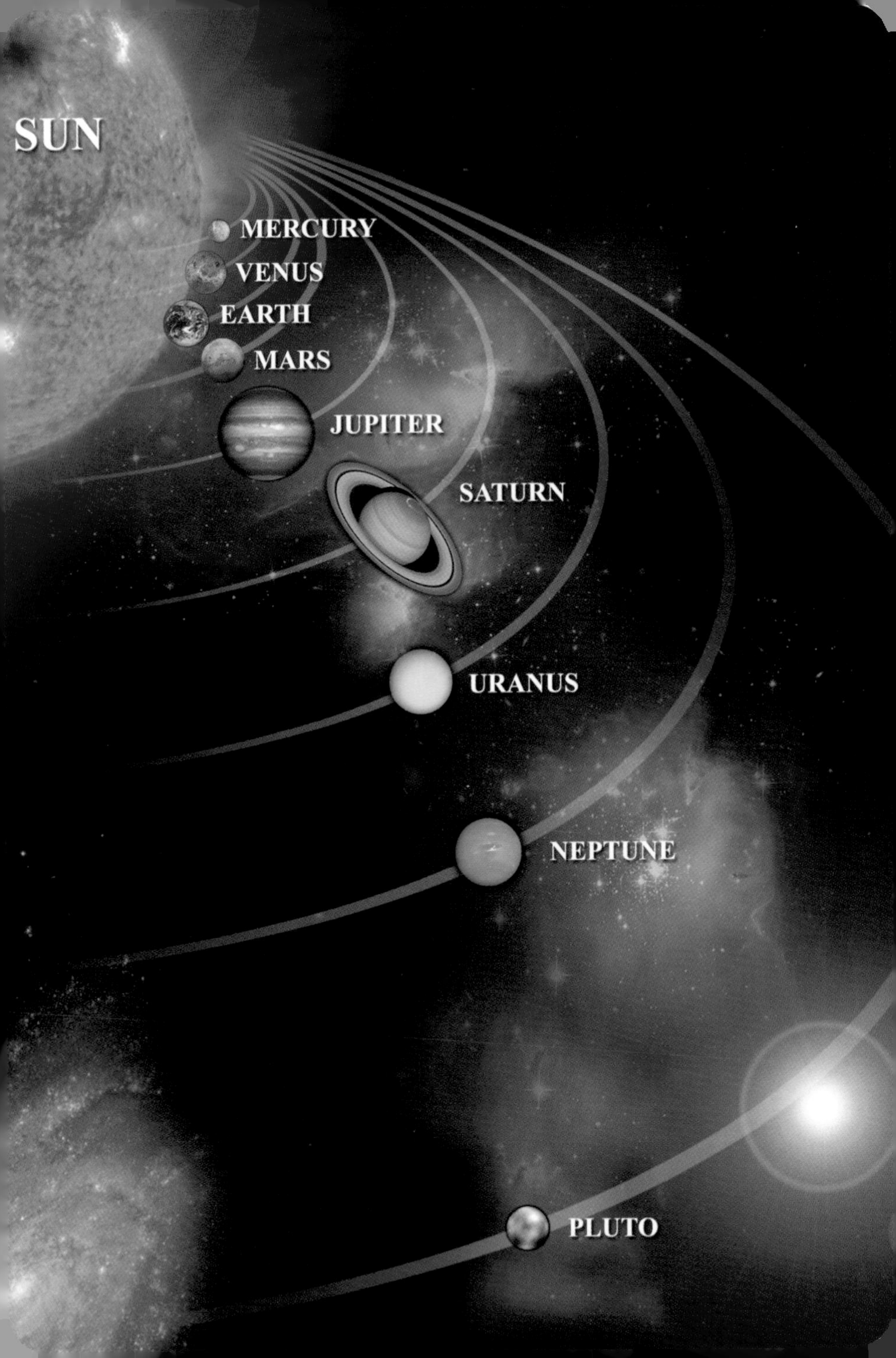
SUN
MERCURY
VENUS
EARTH
MARS
JUPITER
SATURN
URANUS
NEPTUNE
PLUTO

In the Stream of Time

Where are we? In the stream of time, that is. In man's best estimations, the universe as we know it from our vantage point is around 13.7 billion years old. Our Milky Way galaxy is thought to be 13.2 billion years old. Our Sun is considered to be 4.6 billion years old. The Earth began to form shortly thereafter, about 4.54 billion years ago.

According to the big bang theory, this Grand Universe we have just begun to discover through the use of our collective imaginations, was conceived in 1 Plank unit of time from some sort of subatomic seed compacted with dynamic energy of an unknown nature and incomprehensible to man. If the theory holds true, it is at that moment of conception, or germination, or whatever term you want to use short of miracle, a Grand Universe was born which has blossomed forth, stars without number, collecting into massive black holes to become the central powerhouse for galaxies that, in turn, have given birth to billions of other stars, who, in their turn, have birthed planets and other cosmic phenomenon.

The all-inclusive *incomparable energy* that powers all the heavenly bodies in the Universe is a power beyond man's ability to understand. The only term in our human vocabulary that can come close to describing it is *Supernatural.*

Regardless of one's personal beliefs or religious convictions, this *scientific fact* gives us reason to consider the implications of Isaiah's ancient statement: *"He brings them out like an army, one after another, calling each by its name. Because of his great power and incomparable strength, not a single one is missing."*

The outgrowth of matter from the early universe led to the formation of our solar system, where we now find ourselves some 13.7 billion years later. As caretakers of a planet 4.54 billion years old, with a recorded human history of just over 5,500 years, we have just begun our journey. We are but babes in the grand stream of time. Where do we go from here?

We are physical beings in a universe perfectly suited for us; but we struggle to know why we are here. In many ways, we are being tested on our ability to respect and manage this gift we call Earth. Only through using our collective imaginations—for good all the time and for the benefit of all—can we go forward and finish the work we have to do on Earth, before moving on.

There exists no physical thing that does not serve some purpose. The Designer of the planets in our solar system and across the universe surely had a Grand Purpose in mind for them and us when we were placed right in the middle of it all.

Now, to the question: Where are we in the stream of time? Right where we are supposed to be, at the beginning of a wonderful journey, a journey where our imaginations will likely compel us to go forward by some future means into an amazing universe, *made just for us,* in our quest for knowledge and a sense of purpose!

Imagine—A Perfect World!

If you could imagine a perfect world, what would it look like? Perhaps this world is what you would see.

Imagine—an Earth with no holes in the ozone where poisonous radiation is pouring in to harm you. There are no clouds of smoke and poisonous gases spewing from smokestacks or motorized vehicles. There are no global warming issues to worry about because the environment is perfect. The air we breathe is clean and pure once again, with no more smog. You can see the stars clearly when you look up at the night sky. The polar ice caps are stable and no longer in danger of melting. There are no harsh climate conditions caused by unnatural global changes.

Imagine—the world's oceans have been cleaned up from all the pollution that has been dumped into them. The water is crystal clear once again, no more murky water to swim in. The coral reefs have all been restored to their original beautiful condition. There is no more red tide or other conditions that kill sea life. All the species once near extinction are flourishing again. The oceans are teeming with an ideal balance of sea creatures of every kind. Dolphins and other fish are no longer caught up in nets, nor do they die from consuming plastic and other waste left by humans. No oil spills. The water in all the lakes and rivers is crystal clear and pollution-free. To drink it, all you have to do is reach down and scoop it up with your hands.

Imagine—if man were suddenly removed from the Earth, the Earth's self-cleansing process would kick-in immediately and dramatically. Eventually, over time, the air, lakes, rivers, oceans, and the global environment would be pure and clean once again.

Imagine that. Man is the problem with the Earth's environment! How did things get this way? IMAGINATION—man's misuse of it!

Imagine—a world where there are no more wars and everyone is living in peace. No mothers, fathers, brothers, sisters, wives, husbands, or children having to mourn the loss of their loved ones on the battlefield. No more innocent children maimed or killed from landmines. There are no more nuclear bombs. No more tanks, missiles, or poisonous gas. In fact, there is no longer a need for weapons because all humans respect each other and treat one another like brothers and sisters. Everyone is kind and considerate to each other. The world is a place where we serve one another rather than ourselves. There is no more racial strife or national hatred because all are considered equals. No more political discord or corrupt leaders. There is no more religious conflict or indifference because the world's spirituality is singular.

Imagine—a world where cancer has been cured, heart disease is no more, HIV is a thing of the past. No more blindness, no need for hearing aids, no need for wheelchairs. No more mental illness. Hospitals close down—no more patients, so doctors are unnecessary as well. No one gets sick anymore, that is a thing of the past. There are no more tombstones or graveyards; the dead loved ones you longed for have returned. You get up each day feeling youthful, full of vitality and energy, ready to see what exciting adventures the day will bring.

Imagine—a world where no one is mugged, robbed, or raped. Where children can play safely and not worry about being abducted or molested. There are no drive-by shootings or murders. You don't have to lock your doors because no one will rob you or steal your things. There are no bullies to pick on you or make fun of you. There are no homeless, or children without parents. You do not have to be afraid to walk down a dark street alone, because there is no one to harm you. There are no wives or husbands suffering from spousal abuse. There are no more prisons, because there are no more criminals. There are no more drunk drivers to kill and maim innocent people. No more homes broken from divorce.

Imagine—a world where there is no more famine, no more hunger. There are no children with bloated stomachs dying from malnutrition. There is plenty of nutritious food for everyone to eat. There is an abundant variety and it is all delicious. There is plenty of clean water to drink.

Imagine—there are no more zoos, because the animals roam free. There is no need to cage them because they will not harm you. There are no more animals being senselessly killed. Once endangered animals thrive once again. Children can play with all the animals and not be bitten, mauled, or harmed in any way.

Imagine—a world where the work you do is not drudgery, but a delight, because it is the job of your dreams—your passion. You love your job as a marine biologist, an artist, an entertainer, an astronomer, a musician, a gourmet cook, a teacher, an engineer, or an architect—or all of the above, because time is endless for you. You travel the world and see all there is to see. You take time as you travel to meet every other person on the planet and spend time getting to know them. You love animals, so you take the time to study and learn all there is to know about every animal on the planet. You take the time to explore the oceans and get to know about every single sea creature.

Imagine—a world where the Earth is a base station; the starting point from where human life is spread out into the endless and timeless universe. In this world our collective imagination is used only for the good and benefit of all, and to devise and created previously unimagined means to travel the universe. It is a world where, through the use of imagination, we become caretakers of the worlds beyond this doorway, to populate, beautify, and maintain for eternity with a complete sense of purpose.

Through Imagination we discovered this doorway to a world without boundaries. Can our imagination now be used to bring us a perfect world that will spread throughout the universe for all eternity? Our first step to this reality is Imagination. Only when all of Earth's inhabitants can imagine a perfect world, will a perfect world become a reality!

What Does It All Mean?

Yes, as Einstein stated, imagination is everything. It is the preview of life's coming attractions. What can we conclude? What does it all mean? Is there a bigger picture for us to see? Since truth is that which conforms to fact or reality, to answer those questions we must look at the facts. From what we have discovered beyond this doorway, the evidence is clear that there exists an incomparable power source that has created all the stars, just as the ancient prophet Isaiah stated long before the telescope was invented.

Even though this incomparable power source is beyond our comprehension, it is not beyond our imagination. Even though it is beyond our comprehension that this power source surely has always existed, that, too, is not beyond our imagination. The fact that, as humans, we possess an imagination that serves as the driving force we use to create and shape our future and envision life's coming attractions, is in and of itself a simple truth that reveals we and the universe around us could only have come about through the same process of imagination but from one of a far superior degree (Imagination Supreme).

The evidence and our makeup show we were formed from the Earth. The discoveries revealed beyond this Secret Doorway, by Hubble, Spitzer and other telescopes, show the Earth was formed from our Sun; our Sun, in turn, was formed from the Milky Way galaxy; the Milky Way galaxy was formed from stars in the universe; and the universe was formed according to the big bang theory, from an incomparable source of energy. We do not have full comprehension of any of these acts of Supreme Creative Imagination, but we have used our imaginations to accept the evidence and findings we have discovered thus far.

Even though we cannot fully comprehend this power source and how the universe came about, we can imagine it. Think about how we each use our creative imagination to envision, create, and bring into existence things that formally did not exist. Your vision of your future creation, be it a painting, an invention, a book, a song, or whatever, starts as a thought process and through the use of your imagination you devise a way to bring your vision to reality. Now, that product or creation can never come into existence on its own. It will not create itself. You have to imagine it. You have to create it. And, you have to make it a reality—it simply will not come about any other way.

Like the creation or product conceived in your mind, the universe could never have come into existence on its own, it could not create itself. Someone with an incomprehensible power and Supreme Imagination had to first envision and imagine it, and then they had to create it and make it a reality. Even though none of us witnessed the invention of fireworks, it does not discard the facts that someone with imagination did it. We have the evidence. The same holds true for the universe. Even though we did not witness the creation of the universe, it does not discard the fact that someone with Supreme imagination did it. We have the evidence now, pouring in from space via flying telescopes. As time marches on, this body of evidence will continue to mount with each generation as we further our quest to know, through the use of imagination

As we now witness this Grand Drama unfold before us, the evidence, the facts, and the reality lead to this important conclusion: What Isaiah must have imagined on that starry night as he looked up into the heavens and pondered the profound words he wrote was, "This statement is TRUTH!"

> *"To whom will you compare me? Who is my equal? asks the Holy One. Look up into the heavens. Who created all the stars? He brings them out like an army, one after another, calling each by its name. Because of his great power and incomparable strength, not a single one is missing."*

The words he penned so long ago, go to the very core of our existence. After looking into this intriguing thing we call imagination, perhaps you feel as did Sir Isaac Newton when he said, "This most beautiful system [The Universe] could only proceed from the counsel and dominion of an intelligent Being."(1643–1727) Have we, perhaps, been drawn to this Secret Doorway beyond imagination by the One who created all the stars in order to show us His incomparable power and Imagination? Is there a bigger purpose He wants to show us beyond this Earth to expand our imagination forever?

No matter what our personal beliefs are ,we all face the choice to believe it or not, that we are the product of Supreme Imagination; it is through this same process that we each, in our own way, shape the world around us through the things we create. It is through this same imagination that we will be compelled to find a way to explore the universe in the future in ways unimagined and impossible today. It is through the use of imagination that we now find ourselves peering through a once Secret Doorway to witness the Grandest Drama ever to unfold before human eyes—the incredible creation of Heaven and Earth!

Like wide-eyed young children we now find ourselves seated in the theater of imagination in awe of every scene as each inspiring frame is transmitted from space to complete the reel of this silent motion picture. We don't fully comprehend for now what is unfolding on the screen before us, or what it all means, because the drama is not yet over and there are still many scenes yet to come.

As man is drawn forward into the future by his bold quest for knowledge and a sense of purpose, the pieces to life's puzzle will come together, and as the big picture emerges, he will finally understand his purpose in this vast and wonderful place he has just discovered—**Our Incredible Universe.**

Imagination is the Secret Doorway to our future.

About This Heavenly Art Gallery

On the following pages you will view the artwork of the Grandest Artist ever known, whose works, until recently, were unknown! It is truly out of this world and a grand reflection of Supreme Power, Wisdom, Artistic Genius, and Creative Imagination—beyond human comprehension. These works of cosmic art tell a story of our past, including the creation of man's existence on Earth.

How did these Heavenly works of art come about? Common logic dictates that, as with any great work of art, imagination played a key role; in this case, Supreme Imagination had to have been used. And it required expended effort and energy on the part of the designer—in this case, Dynamic Energy beyond belief.

These works of art were not painted by mere mortals with brush strokes of colored oil paints onto cloth canvases. No, they were painted with cosmic dust supercharged with dynamic energy onto a canvas of dark energy peppered with stars covering billions of light-years across the great expanse of the heavens—truly a living orchestra playing in symphony.

In likeness of this Supreme Architect, man has been given the wonderful gift of creative imagination and, thus, we can now view this exquisite collection through space telescopes, like an unfolding Drama, perhaps in response to that invitation from 2,700 years ago. No other generation has been given such a peek into the mind of Imagination Supreme. Realize, that as beautiful as these images are, they are mere reflections of the reality that are alive, in motion and powered by dynamic energy. This collection is living proof of their Designer's Superior Power, Design, Wisdom, and Imagination.

Hopefully this gallery will inspire you and build your appreciation for the Supreme Imagination demonstrated in these heavenly works of art. Each accompanying page contains information about the image. Also, for a comparison, at the bottom of each page are the names of men and women who have been respected for what they achieved through the use of their creative imaginations and the contributions they made to help shape our small world.

As you look at the awe-inspiring images on the left, compare the creative difference between them and the manmade inventions listed below the text. You will no doubt agree that as creative and important as man's accomplishments are, they pale in comparison to the Supreme Imagination behind these wonderful cosmic works.

"Imagination is everything."

How will we use this curious thing to shape our future?

THE GALLERY

OF A FORMALLY UNKNOWN ARTIST WITH
IMAGINATION SUPREME

Crab Nebula NGC 1952

This is a mosaic image, one of the largest ever taken by NASA's Hubble Space Telescope of the Crab Nebula, a six-light-year-wide expanding remnant of a star's supernova explosion. Japanese and Chinese astronomers recorded this violent event nearly 1,000 years ago in 1054, as did, almost certainly, Native Americans.

The orange filaments are the tattered remains of the star and consist mostly of hydrogen. The rapidly spinning neutron star embedded in the center of the nebula is the dynamo powering the nebula's eerie interior bluish glow. The blue light comes from electrons whirling at nearly the speed of light around magnetic field lines from the neutron star. The neutron star, like a lighthouse, ejects twin beams of radiation that appear to pulse thirty times a second due to the neutron star's rotation. A neutron star is the crushed ultra-dense core of the exploded star.

The Crab Nebula derived its name from its appearance in a drawing made by Irish astronomer Lord Rosse in 1844, using a 36-inch telescope. When viewed by Hubble, as well as by large ground-based telescopes such as the European Southern Observatory's Very Large Telescope, the Crab Nebula takes on a more detailed appearance that yields clues into the spectacular demise of a star 6,500 light-years away.

This composite image of the Crab Nebula uses data from three of NASA's Great Observatories. The Chandra X-ray image is shown in light blue, the Hubble Space Telescope optical images are in green and dark blue, and the Spitzer Space Telescope's infrared image is in red. The size of the X-ray image is smaller than the others because the outwardly streaming higher-energy electrons emitting X-ray light radiate away their energy more quickly than the lower-energy electrons emitting optical and infrared light. The neutron star, which has the mass equivalent to the sun crammed into a rapidly spinning ball of neutrons twelve miles across, is the bright white dot in the center of the image.

The matter from a neutron star is so dense that one teaspoon of matter can weigh as much as 200 million elephants.

Imagination of Man

Great Pyramid of Cheops ~ Egyptian Pharaoh Khufu of the Fourth Dynasty

IMAGINATION SUPREME

Spiral Galaxy NGC 3370

Amid a backdrop of far-off galaxies, the majestic dusty spiral NGC 3370 looms in the foreground in this NASA Hubble Space Telescope image. Recent observations taken with the Advanced Camera for Surveys show intricate spiral arm structure spotted with hot areas of new star formation. But this galaxy is more than just a pretty face. Nearly ten years earlier, NGC 3370, in the constellation Leo, hosted a bright exploding star.

In November 1994, the light of a supernova in nearby NGC 3370 reached Earth. This stellar outburst briefly outshone all of the tens of billions of other stars in its galaxy. Although supernovae are common, with one exploding every few seconds somewhere in the universe, this one was special. Designated SN 1994ae, this supernova was one of the nearest and best observed supernovae since the advent of modern digital detectors. It resides 98 million light-years (30 megaparsecs) from Earth. The supernova was also a member of a special subclass of supernovae, the type Ia, the best tool astronomers have to chart the growth rate of the expanding universe.

Recently, astronomers have compared nearby type Ia supernovae to more distant ones, determining that the universe is now accelerating in its expansion and is filled with mysterious "dark energy." Such measurements are akin to measuring the size of your room by stepping it off with your feet. However, a careful measurement of the length of your foot (to convert your measurements into inches or centimeters) is still needed to know the true size of your room. Similarly, astronomers must calibrate the true brightness of type Ia supernovae to measure the true size and expansion rate of the universe.

The very nearest type Ia supernovae, such as SN 1994ae, can be used to calibrate distance measurements in the universe because other fainter stars of known brightness can be observed in the same galaxy. These stellar "standard candles" are the Cepheid variable stars, which vary regularly in brightness with periods that are directly related to their intrinsic brightness, and thus allow the distance to the galaxy—and the supernova—to be determined directly.

Imagination of Man

Grand Piano ~ Heinrich Engelhard Steinway
(1853)

Star Formation in RCW49

One of the most prolific birthing grounds in our Milky Way galaxy, a nebula called RCW 49 is exposed in superb detail for the first time in this new image from NASA's Spitzer Space Telescope. Located 13,700 light-years away in the southern constellation Centaurus, RCW 49 is a dark and dusty stellar nursery that houses more than 2,200 stars.

Because many of the stars in RCW 49 are deeply embedded in plumes of dust, they cannot be seen at visible wavelengths. When viewed with Spitzer's infrared eyes, however, RCW 49 becomes transparent. Like cracking open a quartz rock to discover its jewels inside, the nebula's newborn stars have been dramatically exposed.

This image taken by Spitzer's infrared array camera highlights the nebula's older stars (blue stars in center pocket), its gas filaments (green), and dusty tendrils (pink). Speckled throughout the murky clouds are more than 300 never-before-seen newborn stars.

Astronomers are interested in further studying these newfound proto-stars because they offer a fresh look at star formation in our own galaxy.

Imagination of Man

Negative/Positive Photographic Process ~ William Tabot
(1840)

Whirlpool Galaxy M51 and Companion Galaxy

The graceful winding arms of the majestic spiral galaxy M51 (NGC 5194) appear like a grand spiral staircase sweeping through space. They are actually long lanes of stars and gas laced with dust. This sharpest-ever image of the Whirlpool Galaxy, taken in January 2005 with the Advanced Camera for Surveys aboard NASA's Hubble Space Telescope, illustrates a spiral galaxy's grand design, from its curving spiral arms, where young stars reside, to its yellowish central core, a home of older stars. The galaxy is nicknamed the Whirlpool because of its swirling structure.

The Whirlpool's most striking feature is its two curving arms, a hallmark of so-called grand-design spiral galaxies. Many spiral galaxies possess numerous loosely shaped arms which make their spiral structure less pronounced. These arms serve an important purpose in spiral galaxies. They are star-formation factories, compressing hydrogen gas and creating clusters of new stars. In the Whirlpool, the assembly line begins with the dark clouds of gas on the inner edge, then moves to bright pink star-forming regions, and ends with the brilliant blue star clusters along the outer edge.

Some astronomers believe that the Whirlpool's arms are so prominent because of the effects of a close encounter with NGC 5195, the small yellowish galaxy at the outermost tip of one of the Whirlpool's arms. At first glance, the compact galaxy appears to be tugging on the arm. Hubble's clear view, however, shows that NGC 5195 is passing behind the Whirlpool. The small galaxy has been gliding past the Whirlpool for hundreds of millions of years.

As NGC 5195 drifts by, its gravitational muscle pumps up waves within the Whirlpool's pancake-shaped disk. The waves are like ripples in a pond generated when a rock is thrown in the water. When the waves pass through orbiting gas clouds within the disk, they squeeze the gaseous material along each arm's inner edge. The dark dusty material looks like gathering storm clouds. These dense clouds collapse, creating a wake of star birth, as seen in the bright pink star-forming regions. The largest stars eventually sweep away the dusty cocoons with a torrent of radiation, hurricane-like stellar winds, and shock waves from supernova blasts. Bright blue star clusters emerge from the mayhem, illuminating the Whirlpool's arms like city streetlights.

The Whirlpool is one of astronomy's galactic darlings. Located 31 million light-years away in the constellation Canes Venatici (the Hunting Dogs), the Whirlpool's beautiful face-on view and closeness to Earth allow astronomers to study a classic spiral galaxy's structure and star-forming processes.

Imagination of Man

Printing Press ~ Johann Gutenberg
(1439)

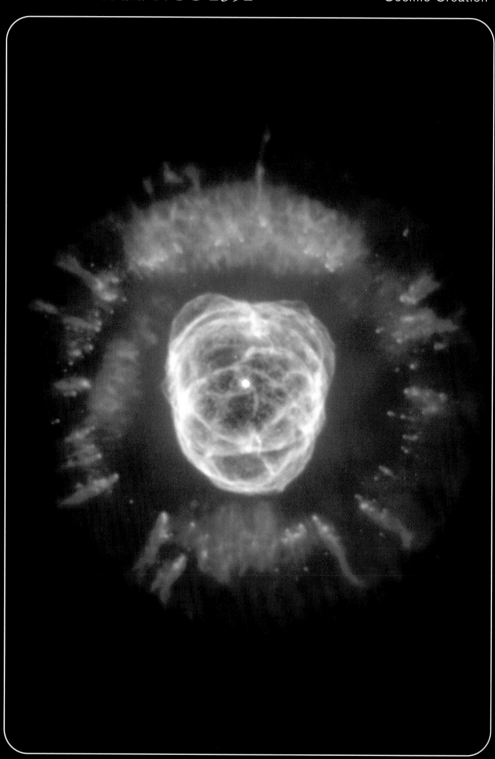

Eskimo Nebula NGC 2392

In its first glimpse of the heavens following the successful December 1999 servicing mission, NASA's Hubble Space Telescope has captured a majestic view of a planetary nebula, the glowing remains of a dying Sun-like star. This stellar relic, first spied by William Herschel in 1787, is nicknamed the "Eskimo" Nebula (NGC 2392) because, when viewed through ground-based telescopes, it resembles a face surrounded by a fur parka. In this Hubble telescope image, the "parka" is really a disk of material embellished with a ring of comet-shaped objects, with their tails streaming away from the central dying star. The Eskimo's "face" also contains some fascinating details. Although this bright central region resembles a ball of twine, it is, in reality, a bubble of material being blown into space by the central star's intense "wind" of high-speed material.

The planetary nebula began forming about 10,000 years ago, when the dying star began flinging material into space. The nebula is composed of two elliptically shaped lobes of matter streaming above and below the dying star. In this photo, one bubble lies in front of the other, obscuring part of the second lobe.

Scientists believe that a ring of dense material around the star's equator, ejected during its red giant phase, created the nebula's shape. This dense waist of material is plodding along at 72,000 miles per hour (115,000 kilometers per hour), preventing high-velocity stellar winds from pushing matter along the equator. Instead, the 900,000-mile-per-hour (1.5-million-kilometer-per-hour) winds are sweeping the material above and below the star, creating the elongated bubbles. The bubbles are not smooth like balloons but have filaments of denser matter. Each bubble is about one light-year long and about half a light-year wide. Scientists are still puzzled about the origin of the comet-shaped features in the "parka." One possible explanation is that these objects formed from a collision of slow- and fast-moving gases.

The Eskimo Nebula is about 5,000 light-years from Earth in the constellation Gemini. The picture was taken January 10 and 11, 2000, with the Wide Field and Planetary Camera 2. The nebula's glowing gases produce the colors in this image: nitrogen (red), hydrogen (green), oxygen (blue), and helium (violet).

Imagination of Man

Calculating Machines ~ Wilhelm Schickard
(1623)

Bubble Nebula NGC 7635

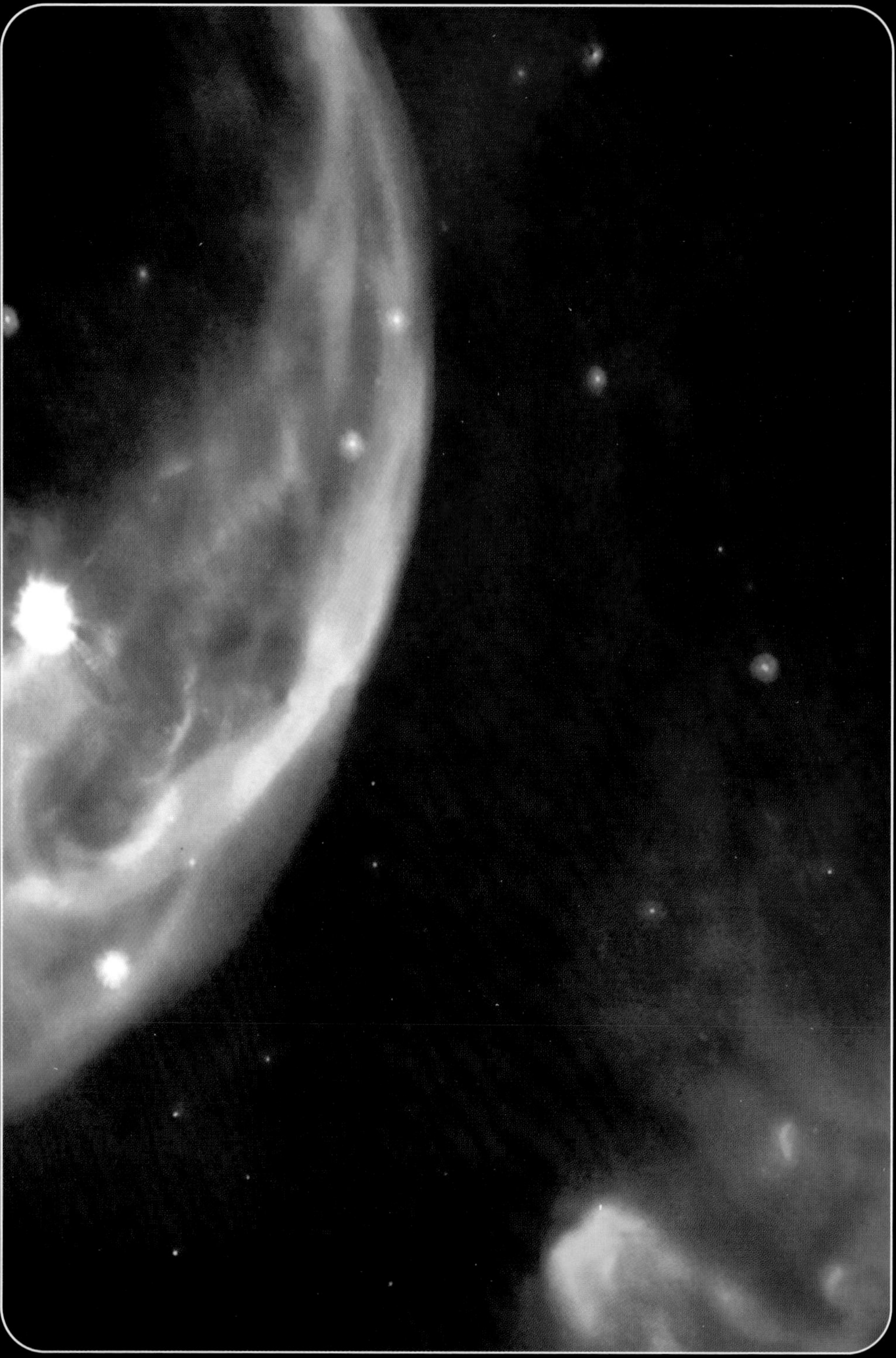

Bubble Nebula NGC 7635

This NASA Hubble Space Telescope image reveals an expanding shell of glowing gas surrounding a hot massive star in our Milky Way galaxy. This shell is being shaped by strong stellar winds of material and radiation produced by the bright star at the left, which is ten to twenty times more massive than our Sun. These fierce winds are sculpting the surrounding material—composed of gas and dust—into the curve-shaped bubble.

Astronomers have dubbed it the Bubble Nebula NGC 7635. The nebula is ten light-years across, more than twice the distance from Earth to the nearest star. Only part of the bubble is visible in this image. The glowing gas in the lower right-hand corner is a dense region of material that is getting blasted by radiation from the Bubble Nebula's massive star. The radiation is eating into the gas, creating finger-like features. This interaction also heats up the gas, causing it to glow.

The remarkably spherical "bubble" marks the boundary between an intense wind of particles from the star and the more quiescent interior of the nebula. The central star of the nebula is forty times more massive than the Sun and is responsible for a stellar wind moving at 2,000 kilometers per second (four million miles per hour or seven million kilometers per hour) which propels particles off the surface of the star. The bubble surface actually marks the leading edge of this wind's gust front, which is slowing as it plows into the denser surrounding material.

The surface of the bubble is not uniform because as the shell expands outward it encounters regions of the cold gas, which are of different density and therefore arrest the expansion by differing amounts, resulting in the rippled appearance. It is this gradient of background material that the wind is encountering that places the central star off center in the bubble. There is more material to the northeast of the nebula than to the southwest, so that the wind progresses less in that direction, offsetting the central star from the geometric center of the bubble. At a distance of 7,100 light-years from Earth, the Bubble Nebula is located in the constellation Cassiopeia and has a diameter of six light-years.

Imagination of Man

Dishwasher ~ Josephine Cochran
(1886)

Elephant's Trunk Nebula

NASA's Spitzer Space Telescope has captured a glowing stellar nursery within a dark globule that is opaque at visible light. These new images pierce through the obscuration to reveal the birth of new protostars, or embryonic stars, and young stars never before seen. The Elephant's Trunk Nebula is an elongated dark globule within the emission nebula IC 1396 in the constellation of Cepheus. Located at a distance of 2,450 light-years, the globule is a condensation of dense gas that is barely surviving the strong ionizing radiation from a nearby massive star. The globule is being compressed by the surrounding ionized gas.

The large composite image on the left is a product of combining data from the observatory's multiband imaging photometer and the infrared array camera. The thermal emission at 24 microns measured by the photometer (red) is combined with near-infrared emission from the camera at 3.6/4.5 microns (blue) and from 5.8/8.0 microns (green). The colors of the diffuse emission and filaments vary, and are a combination of molecular hydrogen (which tends to be green) and polycyclic aromatic hydrocarbon (brown) emissions.

Within the globule, a half dozen newly discovered protostars are easily discernible as the bright red tinted objects, mostly along the southern rim of the globule. These were previously undetected at visible wavelengths due to obscuration by the thick cloud ("globule body") and by dust surrounding the newly forming stars. The newborn stars form in the dense gas because of compression by the wind and radiation from a nearby massive star (located outside the field of view to the left). The winds from this unseen star are also responsible for producing the spectacular filamentary appearance of the globule itself, which resembles that of a flying dragon.

The Spitzer Space Telescope also sees many newly discovered young stars, often enshrouded in dust, which may be starting the nuclear fusion that defines a star. These young stars are too cool to be seen at visible wavelengths. Both the protostars and young stars are bright in the mid-infrared because of their surrounding discs of solid material. A few of the visible light stars in this image were found to have excess infrared emission, suggesting they are more mature stars surrounded by primordial remnants from their formation, or from crumbling asteroids and comets in their planetary systems.

Imagination of Man

The Phonograph ~ Thomas Edison
(1877)

IMAGINATION SUPREME

Orion Nebula M42, NGC 1976

This dramatic image offers a peek inside a cavern of roiling dust and gas where thousands of stars are forming. The image, taken by the Advanced Camera for Surveys (ACS) aboard NASA's Hubble Space Telescope, represents the sharpest view ever taken of this region, called the Orion Nebula. More than 3,000 stars of various sizes appear in this image. Some of them have never been seen in visible light. These stars reside in a dramatic dust-and-gas landscape of plateaus, mountains, and valleys that are reminiscent of the Grand Canyon.

The Orion Nebula is a picture book of star formation, from the massive young stars that are shaping the nebula to the pillars of dense gas that may be the homes of budding stars. The bright central region is the home of the four heftiest stars in the nebula. The stars are called the Trapezium because they are arranged in a trapezoid pattern. Ultraviolet light unleashed by these stars is carving a cavity in the nebula and disrupting the growth of hundreds of smaller stars. Located near the Trapezium stars are stars still young enough to have disks of material encircling them. These disks are called protoplanetary disks or "proplyds" and are too small to see clearly in this image. The disks are the building blocks of solar systems.

The bright glow at the upper left is from M43, a small region being shaped by a massive young star's ultraviolet light. Astronomers call the region a miniature Orion Nebula because only one star is sculpting the landscape. The Orion Nebula has four such stars. Next to M43 are dense dark pillars of dust and gas that point toward the Trapezium. These pillars are resisting erosion from the Trapezium's intense ultraviolet light. The glowing region on the right reveals arcs and bubbles formed when stellar winds—streams of charged particles ejected from the Trapezium stars—collide with material.

The faint red stars near the bottom are the myriad brown dwarfs that Hubble spied for the first time in the nebula in visible light. Sometimes called "failed stars," brown dwarfs are cool objects that are too small to be ordinary stars because they cannot sustain nuclear fusion in their cores the way our Sun does. The dark red column, below left, shows an illuminated edge of the cavity wall. The Orion Nebula is 1,500 light-years away, the nearest star-forming region to Earth

Imagination of Man

The *Mona Lisa* ~ Leonardo da Vinci
(1519)

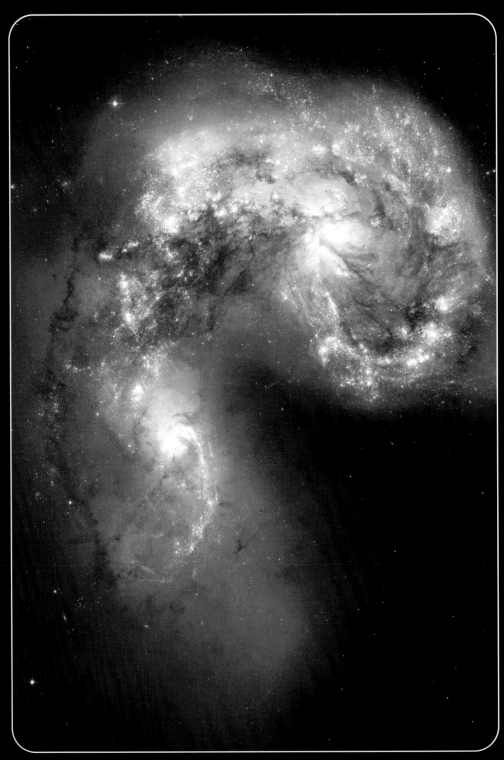

Antennae Galaxies NGC 4038-4039

This new NASA Hubble Space Telescope image of the Antennae Galaxies is the sharpest yet of this merging pair of galaxies. During the course of the collision, billions of stars will be formed. The brightest and most compact of these star birth regions are called "super star clusters".

The two spiral galaxies started to interact a few hundred million years ago, making the Antennae Galaxies one of the nearest and youngest examples of a pair of colliding galaxies. Nearly half of the faint objects in the Antennae image are young clusters containing tens of thousands of stars. The orange blobs to the left and right of the image center are the two cores of the original galaxies and consist mainly of old stars crisscrossed by filaments of dust, which appears brown in the image. The two galaxies are dotted with brilliant blue star-forming regions surrounded by glowing hydrogen gas, appearing in the image in pink.

The new image allows astronomers to better distinguish between the stars and super-star clusters created in the collision of two spiral galaxies. By age-dating the clusters in the image, astronomers find that only about ten percent of the newly formed super-star clusters in the Antennae will survive beyond the first ten million years. The vast majority of the super-star clusters formed during this interaction will disperse, with the individual stars becoming part of the smooth background of the galaxy. It is believed, however, that about a hundred of the most massive clusters will survive to form regular globular clusters, similar to the globular clusters found in our own Milky Way galaxy.

The Antennae Galaxies take their name from the long antenna-like "arms" extending far out from the nuclei of the two galaxies, best seen by ground-based telescopes. These "tidal tails" were formed during the initial encounter of the galaxies some 200 to 300 million years ago. They give us a preview of what may happen when our Milky Way galaxy collides with the neighboring Andromeda galaxy in several billion years.

Imagination of Man

Sundial ~ Anaximander
(611-547)

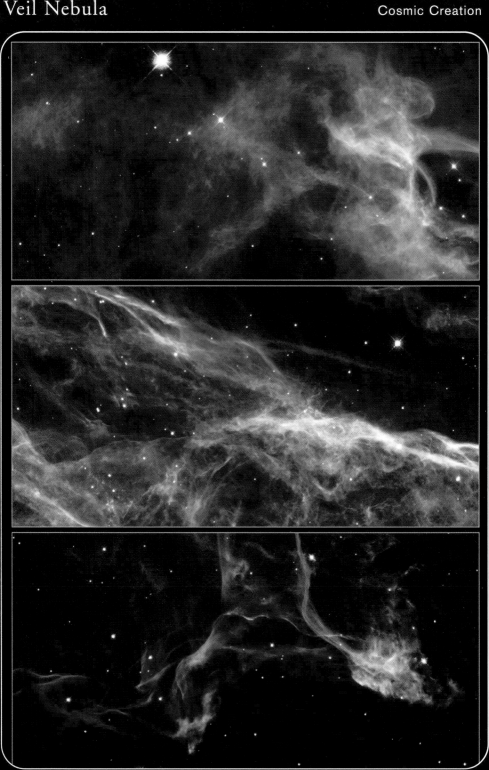

Veil Nebula

NASA's Hubble Space Telescope photographed three magnificent sections of the Veil Nebula—the shattered remains of a supernova that exploded thousands of years ago. This series of images provides beautifully detailed views of the delicate wispy structure resulting from this cosmic explosion. The Veil Nebula is one of the most spectacular supernova remnants. The entire shell spans three degrees on the sky, about six full moons.

The Veil Nebula is a prototypical middle-aged supernova remnant, and is an ideal laboratory for studying the physics of supernova remnants because of its unobscured location in our galaxy, its relative closeness, and its large size. Also known as the Cygnus Loop, the Veil Nebula is located in the constellation of Cygnus, the Swan. It is 1,500 light-years away from Earth.

Stars in our galaxy, and others, are born and then die. How long a star lives depends on how massive it is. The more massive the star, the shorter its life. When a star significantly larger than our Sun runs out of fuel, it collapses and blows itself apart in a catastrophic supernova explosion. A supernova releases so much light that it can outshine a whole galaxy of stars put together. The exploding star sweeps out a huge bubble in its surroundings, fringed with actual stellar debris along with material swept up by the blast wave. This glowing, brightly colored shell of gas forms a nebula that astronomers call a "supernova remnant." Such a remnant can remain visible long after the initial explosion fades away. Scientists estimate that the Veil supernova explosion occurred some 5,000 to 10,000 years ago.

The small regions captured in these Hubble images provide stunning close-ups of the Veil. Fascinating smoke-like wisps of gas are all that remain visible of what was once a star in our Milky Way galaxy. The intertwined rope-like filaments of gas in the Veil Nebula result from the enormous amounts of energy released as the fast-moving debris from the explosion plows into its surroundings and creates shock fronts. These shocks, driven by debris moving at 600,000 kilometers per hour, heat the gas to millions of degrees. It is the subsequent cooling of this material that produces the brilliant glowing colors.

Although only about one star per century in our galaxy will end its life in this spectacular way, these explosions are responsible for making all chemical elements heavier than iron, as well as being the main producers of oxygen, in the universe. Elements such as copper, mercury, gold, and lead are forged in these violent events. The expanding shells of supernova remnants mix with other clouds in the Milky Way and become the raw material for new generations of stars and planets. The chemical elements that constitute Earth, and indeed those of which we ourselves are made, were formed deep inside ancient stars and distributed by supernova explosions in nebulae like the one we see here.

Imagination of Man

Romeo and Juliet ~ William Shakespeare (1591-1595)

Barred Spiral Galaxy NGC 1300

One of the largest Hubble Space Telescope images ever made of a complete galaxy has just been unveiled at the American Astronomical Society meeting in San Diego, California. The Hubble telescope captured a display of starlight, glowing gas, and silhouetted dark clouds of interstellar dust in this four-foot by eight-foot image of the Barred Spiral Galaxy NGC 1300. NGC 1300 is considered to be prototypical of barred spiral galaxies. Barred spirals differ from normal spiral galaxies in that the arms of the galaxy do not spiral all the way into the center, but are connected to the two ends of a straight bar of stars containing the nucleus at its center.

At Hubble's resolution, a myriad of fine details, some of which have never before been seen, can be glimpsed throughout the galaxy's arms, disk, bulge, and nucleus. Blue and red supergiant stars, star clusters, and star-forming regions are well resolved across the spiral arms, and dust lanes trace out fine structures in the disk and bar. Numerous more distant galaxies are visible in the background, and are seen even through the densest regions of NGC 1300.

In the core of the larger spiral structure of NGC 1300, the nucleus shows its own extraordinary and distinct "grand-design" spiral structure that is about 3,300 light-years (1 kiloparsec) long. Only galaxies with large-scale bars appear to have these grand-design inner disks—a spiral within a spiral. Models suggest that the gas in a bar can be funneled inward, and then spiral into the center through the grand-design disk, where it can potentially fuel a central black hole. NGC 1300 is not known to have an active nucleus, however, indicating either that there is no black hole or that it is not accreting matter.

The image was constructed from exposures taken in September 2004 by the Advanced Camera for Surveys onboard Hubble in four filters. Starlight and dust are seen in blue, visible, and infrared light. Bright star clusters are highlighted in red by their associated emission from glowing hydrogen gas. Due to the galaxy's large size, two adjacent pointings of the telescope were necessary to cover the extent of the spiral arms. The galaxy lies roughly sixty-nine million light-years away (twenty-one mega-parsecs) in the direction of the constellation Eridanus.

Imagination of Man

Double-Action Pedal Harp ~ Sebastian Erard
(1801)

Pleiades Star Cluster M45

The brilliant stars seen in this image are members of the popular open star cluster known as the Pleiades, or Seven Sisters. About 1,000 stars comprise the cluster, located in the constellation Taurus.

Astronomers using NASA's Hubble Space Telescope have helped settle a mystery that has puzzled scientists concerning the exact distance to the famous nearby star cluster known as the Pleiades, or the Seven Sisters. The Pleiades cluster, named by the ancient Greeks, is easily seen as a small grouping of stars lying near the shoulder of Taurus, the Bull, in the winter sky. Although it might be expected that the distance to this well-studied cluster would be well established, there has been an ongoing controversy among astronomers about its distance for the past seven years.

The mystery began in 1997, when the European Space Agency's satellite, Hipparcos, measured the distance to the Pleiades and found it was ten percent closer to Earth than traditional estimates, which had been based on comparing the Pleiades to nearby stars. If the Hipparcos measurements were correct, then the stars in the Pleiades are peculiar because they are fainter than Sun-like stars would be at that distance. This finding, if substantiated, would challenge our basic understanding of the structure of stars.

But measurements made by the Hubble telescope's "fine guidance sensors" showed that the distance to the Pleiades is about 440 light-years from Earth, essentially the same as past distance estimates and differing from the Hipparcos results by more than forty light-years. The new results agree with recent measurements made by astronomers at the California Institute of Technology and NASA's Jet Propulsion Laboratory, both in Pasadena, California. Those astronomers used interferometer measurements from Mt. Wilson and Palomar observatories in California, which found that the star cluster is between 434 and 446 light-years from Earth.

The color-composite image of the Pleiades star cluster was taken by the Palomar's 48-inch Schmidt telescope. The image is from the second Palomar Observatory Sky Survey, and is part of the Digitized Sky Survey. The Pleiades photo was made from three separate images taken in red, green, and blue filters. The separate images were taken between November 5, 1986 and September 11, 1996.

Imagination of Man

Electric Guitar ~ A. de Torres
(1931)

IMAGINATION SUPREME

Reflection Nebula NGC 7129

Out of the dark and dusty cosmos comes an unusual valentine—a stellar nursery resembling a shimmering pink rosebud. This cluster of newborn stars, called a "reflection nebula," was captured by state-of-the-art infrared detectors onboard NASA's new Spitzer Space Telescope, formerly known as the Space Infrared Telescope Facility.

"The picture is more than just pretty," said the principal investigator for the latest observations and an astronomer at the Harvard Smithsonian Center for Astrophysics in Cambridge, Massachusetts. "It helps us understand how stars form in the crowded environments of stellar nurseries."

Located 3,330 light-years away in the constellation Cepheus and spanning ten light-years across, the rosebud-shaped nebula, numbered NGC 7129, is home to some 130 young stars. Our own Sun is believed to have grown up in a similar family setting.

Previous images of NGC 7129 taken by visible telescopes show a smattering of hazy stars spotted against a luminescent cloud. Spitzer, by sensing the infrared radiation or heat of the cluster, produces a much more detailed snapshot. Highlighted in false colors are the hot dust particles and gases, respectively, which form a nest around the stars. The pink rosebud contains adolescent stars that blew away blankets of hot dust, while the green stem holds newborn stars whose jets torched surrounding gases.

Outside of the primary nebula, younger proto-stars can also be seen for the first time. "We can now see a few stars beyond the nebula that were previously hidden in the dark cloud."

In addition, the findings go beyond what can be seen in the image. By analyzing the amount and type of infrared light emitted by nearly every star in the cluster, scientists were able to determine which ones support the swirling rings of debris, called "circumstellar disks," which eventually coalesce to form planets. Roughly half of the stars observed were found to harbor disks.

These observations will ultimately help astronomers determine how stellar nurseries shape the development of planetary systems similar to our own.

Imagination of Man

Liquid Fuel Rockets ~ Robert Goddard
(1926)

Moon's View From Columbia

From time to time men and women risk their lives for what they love and believe in. They have such a passion for what they do it is as if they are pulled by some uncontrollable magnetic force that draws them in. Many times, even if they make attempts to escape it, the attraction is too strong and too irresistible. Through their imagination they can see what others cannot envision. It is that small voice within them that keeps pushing them, whispering: "You can do it, don't give up, ignore what they are saying, take the risk, just go for it." When things go wrong, and they do, we can't fault them, because they were compelled beyond their ability to turn back.

In their quest to explore and understand the universe, the crew members of the Space Shuttle Columbia lost their lives after they recorded this digital photo of the moon on their final mission. On February 1, 2003, the shuttle broke up on re-entry into the Earth's atmosphere. Perhaps, as they looked upon this awe-inspiring view of the moon for the final time they felt a since of awe toward the one whose imagination was responsible for this inspiring view.

Their love for space exploration and their quest to respond to the invitation uttered so long ago *"Look up into the heavens. Who created all the stars?"* ultimately cost them their lives, but their lives were not lost in vain. It is through the tireless dedication of them and others like them that we have been given this glimpse into the mind of Imagination Supreme. Without their efforts, this wonderful Gallery of Cosmic Creations to inspire us and build our appreciation for the heavens above, and their Designer would not be possible. It is through their dedication and pioneering of space that we now have a front row seat of the Grandest Drama to ever unfold before human eyes!

Imagination of Man

Space Shuttle ~ NASA
(1981)

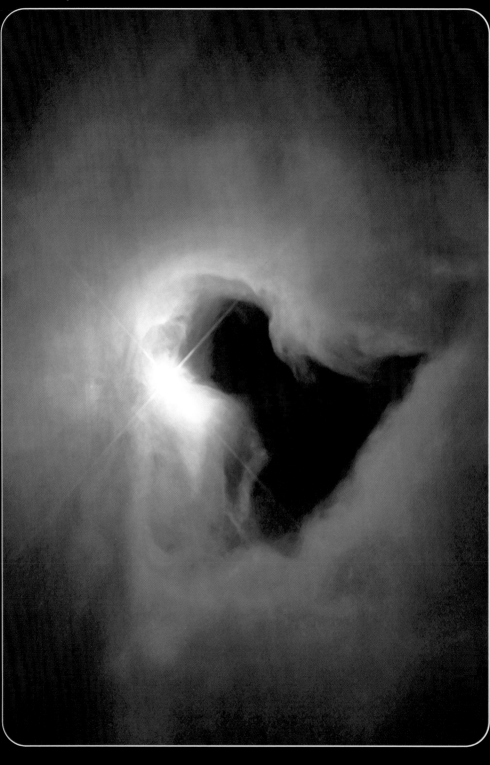

Reflection Nebula NGC 1999

Just weeks after NASA astronauts repaired the Hubble Space Telescope in December 1999, the Hubble Heritage Project snapped this picture of NGC 1999, a nebula in the constellation Orion. NGC 1999 is an example of a reflection nebula. Like fog around a street lamp, a reflection nebula shines only because the light from an embedded source illuminates its dust; the nebula does not emit any visible light of its own. NGC 1999 lies close to the famous Orion Nebula, about 1,500 light-years from Earth, in a region of our Milky Way galaxy where new stars are being formed actively. The nebula is famous in astronomical history because the first Herbig-Haro object was discovered immediately adjacent to it (it lies just outside the new Hubble image). Herbig-Haro objects are now known to be jets of gas ejected from very young stars.

The NGC 1999 nebula is illuminated by a bright recently-formed star, visible in the Hubble photo just to the left of center. This star is cataloged as V380 Orionis, and its white color is due to its high surface temperature of about 10,000 degrees Celsius (nearly twice that of our own Sun). Its mass is estimated to be 3.5 times that of the Sun. The star is so young that it is still surrounded by a cloud of material left over from its formation, here seen as the NGC 1999 reflection nebula.

The WFPC2 image of NGC 1999 shows a remarkable jet-black cloud near its center, resembling the letter "T" tilted on its side, located just to the right and lower right of the bright star. This dark cloud is an example of a "Bok globule," named after the late University of Arizona astronomer Bart Bok. The globule is a cold cloud of gas, molecules, and cosmic dust, which is so dense it blocks all of the light behind it. In the Hubble image, the globule is seen silhouetted against the reflection nebula illuminated by V380 Orionis. Astronomers believe that new stars may be forming inside Bok globules through the contraction of the dust and molecular gas under their own gravity.

NGC 1999 was discovered some two centuries ago by Sir William Herschel and his sister Caroline, and was catalogued later in the 19th century as object 1999 in the New General Catalogue.

Imagination of Man

Airplane ~ Orville & Wilbur Wright
(1903)

Orion Nebula M24, NGC 1976

A new image from NASA's Spitzer and Hubble Space Telescope looks more like an abstract painting than a cosmic snapshot. The magnificent masterpiece shows the Orion nebula in an explosion of infrared, ultraviolet, and visible-light colors. It was "painted" by hundreds of baby stars on a canvas of gas and dust, with intense ultraviolet light and strong stellar winds as brushes.

At the heart of the artwork is a set of four monstrously massive stars, collectively called the Trapezium. These behemoths are approximately 100,000 times brighter than our Sun. Their community can be identified as the yellow smudge near the center of the composite.

The swirls of green were revealed by Hubble's ultraviolet and visible-light detectors. They are hydrogen and sulfur gases heated by intense ultraviolet radiation from the Trapezium's stars.

Wisps of red, also detected by Spitzer, indicate infrared light from illuminated clouds containing carbon-rich molecules called "polycyclic aromatic hydrocarbons." On Earth, polycyclic aromatic hydrocarbons are found on burnt toast and in automobile exhaust.

Additional stars in Orion are sprinkled throughout the image in a rainbow of colors. Spitzer exposed infant stars deeply embedded in a cocoon of dust and gas (orange-yellow dots). Hubble found less embedded stars (specks of green) and stars in the foreground (blue). Stellar winds from clusters of newborn stars scattered throughout the cloud etched all of the well-defined ridges and cavities.

Located 1,500 light-years away from Earth, the Orion nebula is the brightest star in the Sword of the Hunter constellation. The cosmic cloud is also our closest massive star-formation factory, and astronomers suspect that it contains about 1,000 young stars.

The Orion constellation can be seen in the fall and winter night skies from northern latitudes. The constellation's nebula is invisible to the unaided eye, but can be resolved with binoculars or small telescopes.

Imagination of Man

Diesel Engine ~ Rudolf Diesel
(1897)

Cosmic Creation

IMAGINATION SUPREME

Small Magellanic Cloud NGC 602

This new image taken with NASA's Hubble Space Telescope depicts bright, blue, newly formed stars that are blowing a cavity in the center of a star-forming region in the Small Magellanic Cloud. At the heart of the star-forming region lies star cluster NGC 602.

The high-energy radiation blazing out from the hot young stars is sculpting the inner edge of the outer portions of the nebula, slowly eroding it away and eating into the material beyond. The diffuse outer reaches of the nebula prevent the energetic outflows from streaming away from the cluster.

Ridges of dust and gaseous filaments are seen towards the northwest (in the upper-left part of the image) and towards the southeast (in the lower right-hand corner). Elephant trunk-like dust pillars point toward the hot blue stars and are telltale signs of their eroding effect. In this region it is possible with Hubble to trace how the star formation started at the center of the cluster and propagated outward, with the youngest stars still forming today along the dust ridges.

The Small Magellanic Cloud in the constellation Tucana is roughly 200,000 light-years from the Earth. Its proximity to us makes it an exceptional laboratory to perform in-depth studies of star formation processes and their evolution in an environment slightly different from our own Milky Way.

Dwarf galaxies, such as the Small Magellanic Cloud, with significantly fewer stars compared to our own galaxy, are considered to be the primitive building blocks of larger galaxies. The study of star formation within this dwarf galaxy is particularly interesting to astronomers because its primitive nature means that it lacks a large percentage of the heavier elements that are forged in successive generations of stars through nuclear fusion.

These observations were taken with Hubble's Advanced Camera for Surveys in July 2004.

Filters that isolate visible and infrared light were combined with a filter that samples the hydrogen and nitrogen emission from the glowing clouds.

Imagination of Man

Television ~ John Logie Baird
(1923)

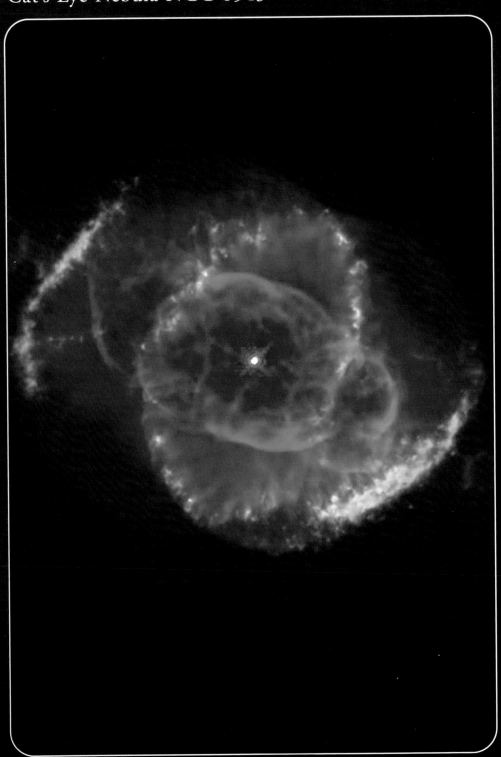

IMAGINATION SUPREME

Cat's Eye Nebula NGC 6543

This NASA Hubble Space Telescope image shows one of the most complex planetary nebulae ever seen, NGC 6543, nicknamed the "Cat's Eye Nebula." Hubble reveals surprisingly intricate structures, including concentric gas shells, jets of high-speed gas, and unusual shock-induced knots of gas. Estimated to be 1,000 years old, the nebula is a visual "fossil record" of the dynamics and late evolution of a dying star.

A preliminary interpretation suggests that the star might be a double-star system. The dynamic effects of two stars orbiting one another most easily explains the intricate structures, which are much more complicated than features seen in most planetary nebulae. (The two stars are too close together to be individually resolved by Hubble, and instead, appear as a single point of light at the center of the nebula.)

According to this model, a fast "stellar wind" of gas blown off the central star created the elongated shell of dense glowing gas. This structure is embedded inside two larger lobes of gas blown off the star at an earlier phase. These lobes are "pinched" by a ring of denser gas, presumably ejected along the orbital plane of the binary companion.

The suspected companion star also might be responsible for a pair of high-speed jets of gas that lie at right angles to this equatorial ring. If the companion was pulling in material from a neighboring star, jets escaping along the companion's rotation axis could be produced.

These jets would explain several puzzling features along the periphery of the gas lobes. Like a stream of water hitting a sand pile, the jets compress gas ahead of them, creating the curlicue features and bright arcs near the outer edge of the lobes. The twin jets are now pointing in different directions than these features. This suggests the jets are wobbling and turning on and off episodically.

This color picture, taken with the Wide Field Planetary Camera-2, is a composite of three images taken at different wavelengths. (red, hydrogen-alpha; blue, neutral oxygen, 6300 angstroms; green, ionized nitrogen, 6584 angstroms). The image was taken on September 18, 1994. NGC 6543 is 3,000 light-years away in the northern constellation Draco.

The term *planetary nebula* is a misnomer; dying stars create these cocoons when they lose outer layers of gas. The process has nothing to do with planet formation, which is predicted to happen early in a star's life.

Imagination of Man

Audiotape Recording ~ Valdemar Poulsen
(1898)

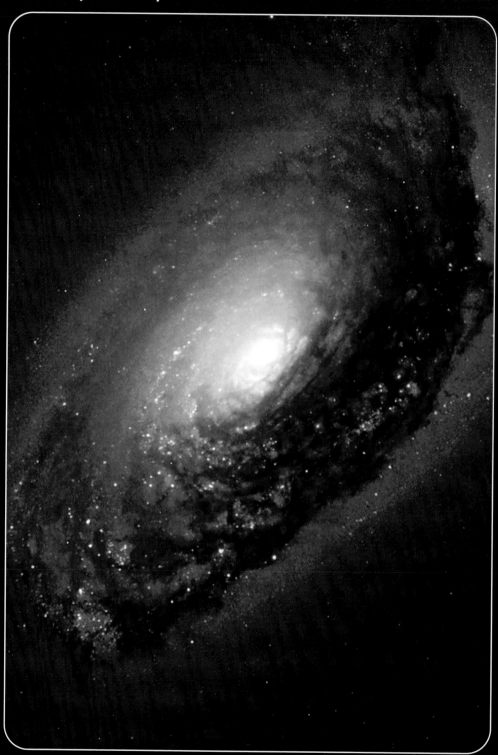

Black Eye Galaxy M64

A collision of two galaxies has left a merged star system with an unusual appearance as well as bizarre internal motions. Messier 64 (M64) has a spectacular dark band of absorbing dust in front of the galaxy's bright nucleus, giving rise to its nicknames of the "Black Eye" or "Evil Eye" galaxy.

Fine details of the dark band are revealed in this image of the central portion of M64 obtained with the Hubble Space Telescope. M64 is well known among amateur astronomers because of its appearance in small telescopes. It was first catalogued in the eighteenth century by the French astronomer Messier. Located in the northern constellation Coma Berenices, M64 resides roughly seventeen million light-years from Earth.

At first glance, M64 appears to be a fairly normal pinwheel-shaped spiral galaxy. As in the majority of galaxies, all of the stars in M64 are rotating in the same direction, clockwise, as seen in the Hubble image. However, detailed studies in the 1990s led to the remarkable discovery that the interstellar gas in the outer regions of M64 rotates in the opposite direction from the gas and stars in the inner regions.

Active formation of new stars is occurring in the shear region where the contrarily rotating gases collide, are compressed, and contract. Particularly noticeable in the image are hot, blue, young stars that have just formed, along with pink clouds of glowing hydrogen gas that fluoresce when exposed to ultraviolet light from newly formed stars.

Astronomers believe that the oppositely rotating gas arose when M64 absorbed a satellite galaxy that collided with it, perhaps more than one billion years ago. This small galaxy has now been almost completely destroyed, but signs of the collision persist in the backward motion of gas at the outer edge of M64.

Imagination of Man

Communication Satellites ~ Soviet Union
(1957)

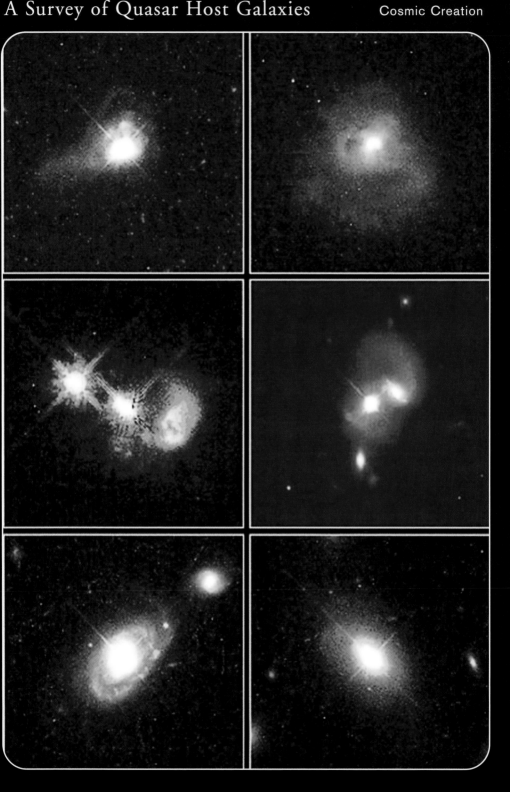

A Survey of Quasar Host Galaxies

Quasars reside in a variety of galaxies, from normal to highly disturbed. When seen through ground-based telescopes, these compact enigmatic light sources resemble stars, yet they are billions of light-years away and several hundred billion times brighter than normal stars. The following Hubble Space Telescope images show examples of different home sites of all quasars. But all the sites must provide the fuel to power these unique light beacons. Astronomers believe that a quasar turns on when a massive black hole at the nucleus of a galaxy feeds on gas and stars. As the matter falls into the black hole, intense radiation is emitted. Eventually, the black hole will stop emitting radiation once it consumes all nearby matter. Then it needs debris from a collision of galaxies or another process to provide more fuel. The column of images on the left represents normal galaxies; the center, colliding galaxies; and the right, peculiar galaxies.

Two teams of astronomers are releasing dramatic Hubble Space Telescope images soon, which show that quasars live in a remarkable variety of galaxies, many of which are violently colliding. This complicated picture suggests there may be a variety of mechanisms—some quite subtle—for "turning on" quasars, the universe's most energetic objects.

The Hubble researchers are also intrigued by the fact that the quasars studied do not appear to have obviously damaged the galaxies in which they live. This could mean that quasars are relatively short-lived phenomena which many galaxies, including the Milky Way, experienced long ago.

Discovered only thirty-three years ago, quasars are among the most baffling objects in the universe because of their small size and prodigious energy output. Quasars are not much bigger than Earth's solar system but pour out 100 to 1,000 times as much light as an entire galaxy containing a hundred billion stars.

A super-massive black hole, gobbling up stars, gas and dust, is theorized to be the "engine" powering a quasar. Most astronomers agree an active black hole is the only credible explanation as to how quasars can be so compact, variable, and powerful. Nevertheless, conclusive evidence has been elusive because quasars are so bright they mask any details of the "environment" where they live.

The luminosity of quasars, therefore, is thought to be about two to ten trillion times that of our Sun, or about 100 to 1000 times that of the total light of average giant galaxies like our Milky Way.

Imagination of Man

Telescope ~ Hans Lippershy
(1608)

Star-Forming Rosette Nebula NGC 2244

This infrared image from NASA's Spitzer Space Telescope shows the Rosette nebula, a pretty star-forming region more than 5,000 light-years away in the constellation Monoceros. In optical light, the nebula looks like a rosebud, or the "rosette" adornments that date back to antiquity. But lurking inside this delicate cosmic rosebud are super-hot stars called O-stars, whose radiation and winds have collectively excavated layers of dust (green) and gas away, revealing the cavity of cooler dust (red). Some of the Rosette's O-stars can be seen in the bubble-like red cavity; however, the largest two blue stars in this picture are in the foreground, and not in the nebula itself.

Astronomers have laid down the cosmic equivalent of yellow "caution" tape around super-hot stars, marking the zones where cooler stars are in danger of having their developing planets blasted away.

In a new study from NASA's Spitzer Space Telescope, scientists report the first maps of so-called planetary "danger zones." These are areas where winds and radiation from super-hot stars can strip other young, cooler stars like our Sun of their planet-forming materials. The results show that cooler stars are safe as long as they lie at least 1.6 light-years, or nearly ten trillion miles, from any hot stars. But cooler stars inside the zone are likely to see their potential planets boiled off into space.

The observations revealed that, beyond ten trillion miles of an O-star, about 45 percent of the stars had disks—about the same amount as there were in safer neighborhoods free of O-stars. Within this distance, only 27 percent of the stars had disks, with fewer and fewer disks spotted around stars closest to the O-star. In other words, an O-star's danger zone is a sphere whose damaging effects are worst at the core. For reference, our Sun's closest star, a small star called Proxima Centauri, is nearly thirty trillion miles away.

Some astronomers think our Sun was born in a similarly violent neighborhood studded with O-stars before migrating to its present, more spacious, home. If so, it was lucky enough to escape a harrowing ride into any danger zones, or our planets, and life as we know it, would not be here today.

Imagination of Man

Wireless Communication ~ Guglielmo Marconi
(1895)

Earth

Earth, our home planet, is the only planet in our solar system known to harbor life —life that is incredibly diverse. All of the things we need to survive are provided under a thin layer of atmosphere that separates us from the uninhabitable void of space. Earth is made up of complex interactive systems that are often unpredictable. Air, water, land, and life—including humans—combine forces to create a constantly changing world that we are striving to understand.

Viewing Earth from the unique perspective of space provides the opportunity to see Earth as a whole. Scientists around the world have discovered many things about our planet by working together and sharing their findings. Some facts are well known. For instance, Earth is the third planet from the Sun and the fifth largest in the solar system. Earth's diameter is just a few hundred kilometers larger than that of Venus. The four seasons are a result of Earth's axis of rotation being tilted more than 23 degrees.

Oceans at least four kilometers deep cover nearly 70 percent of the Earth's surface. Fresh water exists in the liquid phase only within a narrow temperature span (0 degrees to 100 degrees Celsius). This temperature span is especially narrow when contrasted with the full range of temperatures found within the solar system. The presence and distribution of water vapor in the atmosphere is responsible for much of Earth's weather. Near the surface, an ocean of air that consists of 78 percent nitrogen, 21 percent oxygen, and 1 percent other ingredients envelops us. This atmosphere affects Earth's long-term climate and short-term local weather; shields us from nearly all harmful radiation coming from the Sun; and protects us from meteors as well— most of which burn up before they can strike the surface. Satellites have revealed that the upper atmosphere actually swells by day and contracts by night due to solar activity.

Our planet's rapid spin and molten nickel-iron core give rise to a magnetic field, which the solar wind distorts into a teardrop shape. The solar wind is a stream of charged particles continuously ejected from the Sun.

Imagination of Man

Spitzer Space Telescope ~ NASA
(2003)

Cone Nebula NGC 2264

Resembling a nightmarish beast rearing its head from a crimson sea, this monstrous object is actually an innocuous pillar of gas and dust. Called the Cone Nebula (NGC 2264)—so named because, in ground-based images, it has a conical shape—this giant pillar resides in a turbulent star-forming region.

This picture, taken by the newly installed Advanced Camera for Surveys (ACS) aboard NASA's Hubble Space Telescope, shows the upper 2.5 light-years of the nebula, a height that equals twenty-three million roundtrips to the Moon. The entire nebula is seven light-years long. The Cone Nebula resides 2,500 light-years away in the constellation Monoceros.

Radiation from hot young stars (located beyond the top of the image) has slowly eroded the nebula over millions of years. Ultraviolet light heats the edges of the dark cloud, releasing gas into the relatively empty region of surrounding space. There, additional ultraviolet radiation causes the hydrogen gas to glow, which produces the red halo of light seen around the pillar. A similar process occurs on a much smaller scale to gas surrounding a single star, forming the bow-shaped arc seen near the upper left side of the Cone. This arc, seen previously with the Hubble telescope, is sixty-five times larger than the diameter of our solar system. The blue-white light from surrounding stars is reflected by dust. Background stars can be seen peeking through the evaporating tendrils of gas, while the turbulent base is pockmarked with stars reddened by dust.

Over time, only the densest regions of the Cone will be left. Inside these regions, stars and planets may form. The Cone Nebula is a cousin of the M16 pillars, which the Hubble telescope imaged in 1995. Monstrous pillars of cold gas, like the Cone and M16, are common in large regions of star birth. Astronomers believe that these pillars are incubators for developing stars.

Imagination of Man

Geobond ~ Patricia Billings
(1997)

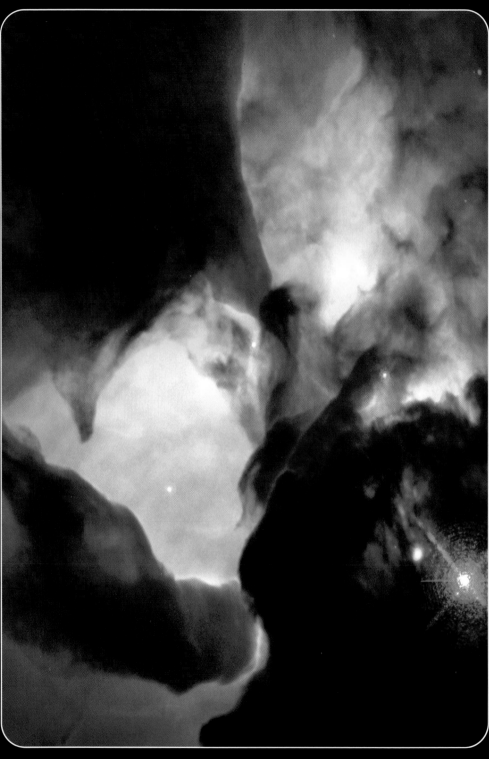

Giant Twisters in the Lagoon Nebula

This NASA Hubble Space Telescope (HST) image reveals a pair of one-half light-year long interstellar "twisters"—eerie funnels and twisted-rope structures—in the heart of the Lagoon Nebula (Messier 8) which lies 5,000 light-years away in the direction of the constellation Sagittarius.

The central hot O-type star, Herschel 36 (lower right), is the primary source of the ionizing radiation for the brightest region in the nebula, called the Hourglass. Other hot stars, also present in the nebula, are ionizing the extended optical nebulosity. The ionizing radiation induces photo-evaporation of the surfaces of the clouds and drives away violent stellar winds tearing into the cool clouds.

Analogous to the spectacular phenomena of Earth tornadoes, the large difference in temperature between the hot surface and cold interior of the clouds, combined with the pressure of starlight, may produce strong horizontal shear to twist the clouds into their tornado-like appearance. Though the spiral shapes suggest the clouds are "twisting," future observations will be needed, perhaps with Hubble's next generation instruments, with the spectroscopic capabilities of the Space Telescope Imaging Spectrograph (STIS) or the Near Infrared Camera and Multi-Object Spectrometer (NICMOS), to actually measure velocities.

The Lagoon Nebula and nebulae in other galaxies are sites where new stars are being born from dusty molecular clouds. These regions are the "space laboratories" for the astronomers to study how stars form and the interactions between the winds from stars and the gas nearby. By studying the wealth of data revealed by HST, astronomers will understand better how stars form in the nebulae.

Imagination of Man

**Computerized Telephone Switching System ~
Erna Schneider Hoover
(1971)**

Mars

The red planet Mars has inspired wild flights of imagination over the centuries, as well as intense scientific interest. Whether fancied to be the source of hostile invaders of Earth, the home of a dying civilization, or a rough-and-tumble mining colony of the future, Mars provides fertile ground for science fiction writers, based on seeds planted by centuries of scientific observations.

We know that Mars is a small rocky body once thought to be very Earth-like. Like the other "terrestrial" planets—Mercury, Venus, and Earth—its surface has been changed by volcanism, impacts from other bodies, movements of its crust, and atmospheric effects such as dust storms. It has polar ice caps that grow and recede with the change of seasons; areas of layered soils near the Martian poles suggest that the planet's climate has changed more than once, perhaps caused by a regular change in the planet's orbit. Martian tectonism—the formation and change of a planet's crust—differs from Earth's. Where Earth tectonics involve sliding plates that grind against each other or spread apart in the seafloors, Martian tectonics seem to be vertical, with hot lava pushing upward through the crust to the surface. Periodically, great dust storms engulf the entire planet. The effects of these storms are dramatic, including giant dunes, wind streaks, and wind-carved features.

Scientists believe that 3.5 billion years ago, Mars experienced the largest known floods in the solar system. This water may even have pooled into lakes or shallow oceans. But where did the ancient flood water come from, how long did it last, and where did it go? In May 2002, scientists announced the discovery of a key piece in the puzzle: the Mars Odyssey spacecraft had detected large quantities of water ice close to the surface—enough to fill Lake Michigan twice over. The ice is mixed into the soil only a meter (about three feet) below the surface of a wide area near the Martian south pole.

Many questions remain. At present, Mars is too cold and its atmosphere is too thin to allow liquid water to exist at the surface for long. More water exists frozen in the polar ice caps, and enough water exists to form ice clouds, but the quantity of water required to carve Mars' great channels and flood plains is not evident on—or near—the surface today. Images from NASA's Mars Global Surveyor spacecraft suggest that underground reserves of water may break through the surface as springs. The answers may lie deep beneath Mars' red soil.

Imagination of Man

Interplanetary Spacecraft ~ NASA
(1962)

Sun

Our solar system's star, the Sun, has inspired mythological stories in cultures around the world, including those of the ancient Egyptians, the Aztecs of Mexico, Native American tribes of North America and Canada, the Chinese, and many others. A number of ancient cultures built stone structures or modified natural rock formations to observe the Sun and Moon, they charted the seasons, created calendars, and monitored solar and lunar eclipses. These architectural sites show evidence of deliberate alignments to astronomical phenomena: sunrises, moonrises, moonsets, even stars or planets.

The Sun is the closest star to Earth, at a mean distance from our planet of 149.60 million kilometers (92.96 million miles). This distance is known as an astronomical unit (abbreviated AU), and sets the scale for measuring distances all across the solar system. The Sun, a huge sphere of mostly ionized gas, supports life on Earth. It powers photosynthesis in green plants and is ultimately the source of all food and fossil fuel. The connection and interactions between the Sun and Earth drive the seasons, ocean currents, weather, and climate. The Sun is 332,900 times more massive than Earth and contains 99.86 percent of the mass of the entire solar system. It is held together by gravitational attraction, producing immense pressure and temperature at its core. The Sun has six regions—the core, the radiative zone, and the convective zone in the interior; the visible surface, known as the photosphere; the chromosphere; and the outermost region, the corona.

At the core, the temperature is about 15 million degrees Celsius (about 27 million degrees Fahrenheit), which is sufficient to sustain thermonuclear fusion. The energy produced in the core powers the Sun and produces essentially all the heat and light we receive on Earth. Energy from the core bounces around the radioactive zone, taking about 170,000 years to get to the convective zone. The temperature drops below 2 million degrees Celsius (3.5 million degrees Fahrenheit) in the convective zone, where large bubbles of hot plasma (a soup of ionized atoms) move upwards.

Imagination of Man

Gasoline Fueled Automobile ~ Karl Benz
(1885)

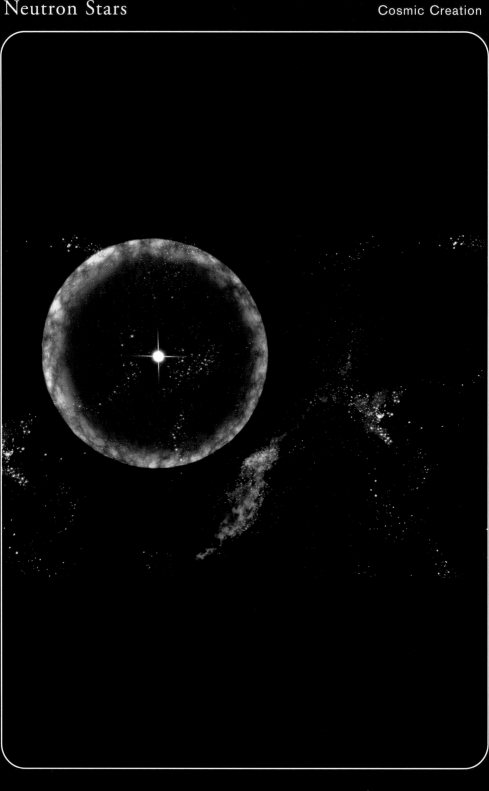

Neutron Stars

Scientists have detected a flash of light from across the Galaxy so powerful that it bounced off the Moon and lit up the Earth's upper atmosphere. The flash was brighter than anything ever detected from beyond our solar system and lasted over a tenth of a second. NASA and European satellites and many radio telescopes detected the flash and its aftermath on December 27, 2004.

The scientists said, as depicted in this artist's concept, that the light came from a "giant flare" on the surface of an exotic neutron star, called a magnetar. The apparent magnitude was brighter than a full moon and all historical star explosions. The light was brightest in the gamma-ray energy range, far more energetic than visible light or X-rays and invisible to our eyes.

A neutron star is about twenty kilometers in diameter and has the mass of about 1.4 times that of our Sun. This means that a neutron star is so dense that on Earth, one teaspoonful would weigh a billion tons! Because of its small size and high density, a neutron star possesses a surface gravitational field about 2×10^{11} times that of Earth. Neutron stars can also have magnetic fields a million times stronger than the strongest magnetic fields produced on Earth.

Neutron stars are one of the possible ends for a star. They result from massive stars which have mass greater than four to eight times that of our Sun. After these stars have finished burning their nuclear fuel, they undergo a supernova explosion. This explosion blows off the outer layers of a star into a beautiful supernova remnant. The central region of the star collapses under gravity. It collapses so much that protons and electrons combine to form neutrons. Hence the name, "neutron star."

Neutron stars may appear in supernova remnants, as isolated objects, or in binary systems. Four neutron stars are thought to have planets. When a neutron star is in a binary system, astronomers are able to measure its mass. From a number of such binaries seen with radio or X-ray telescopes, neutron star masses have been found to be about 1.4 times the mass of the Sun. For binary systems containing an unknown object, this information helps distinguish whether the object is a neutron star or a black hole, since black holes are more massive than neutron stars.

Imagination of Man

Internal Combustion Engine ~ François Isaac de Rivaz
(1806)

Orion Nebula Glass Plume

NASA's Hubble Space Telescope has uncovered the strongest evidence yet that many stars form planetary systems. Scientists from Rice University in Houston, Texas, have used Hubble to discover extended disks of dust around fifteen newly formed stars in the Orion Nebula, a starbirth region 1,500 light-years away. Such disks are a prerequisite for the formation of solar systems like our own. According to the scientists, "These images provide the best evidence for planetary systems. The disks are a missing link in our understanding of how planets like those in our Solar System form. Their discovery establishes that the basic material of planets exists around a large fraction of stars. It is likely that many of these stars will have planetary systems." Hubble Space Telescope's detailed images confirm more than a century of speculation, conjecture, and theory about the genesis of a solar system.

According to current theories, the dust contained within the disks eventually agglomerates to make planets. Our solar system is considered a relic of just such a disk of dust that accompanied our Sun's birth four-and-a-half billion years ago. Before the Hubble discovery, protoplanetary disks had been confirmed around only four stars: Beta Pictoris, Alpha Lyrae, Alpha Piscis Austrini, and Epsilon Eridani. Unlike these previous observations, Hubble has observed newly formed stars less than a million years old which are still contracting out of primordial gas. Hubble's images provide direct evidence that dust surrounding a newborn star has too much spin to be drawn into the collapsing star. Instead the material spreads out into a broad flattened disk.

These young disks signify an entirely new class of object uncovered in the universe. Hubble can see the disks because they are illuminated by the hottest stars in the Orion Nebula; some of them are seen in silhouette against the bright nebula. However, some of these proplyds are bright enough to have been seen previously by ground-based optical and radio telescopes as stars. Their true nature was not recognized until the Hubble discovery. Each proplyd appears as a thick disk with a hole in the middle where the cool star is located. Radiation from nearby hot stars "boils off" material from the disk's surface (at the rate of about one half the mass of our Earth per year). This material is then blown back into a comet-like tail by a stellar "wind" of radiation and subatomic particles streaming from nearby hot stars.

The region of Orion studied intensely by scientists is a bright part of the nebula where stars are being uncovered at the highest rate. These results suggest that nearly half the fifty stars in this part of Orion have protoplanetary disks.

Imagination of Man

Kevlar ~ Stephanie Kwolek
(1966)

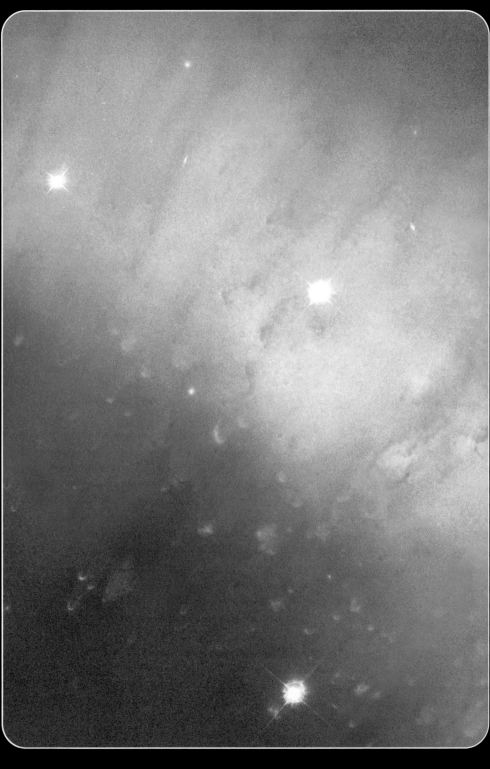

Helix Nebula NGC 7293

This cropped version of the Helix Nebula mosaic shows cometary-filaments embedded along a portion of the inner rim of the nebula's red and blue gas ring. At a distance of 650 light-years, the Helix is one of the nearest planetary nebulae to Earth.

The composite picture is a seamless blend of ultra-sharp NASA Hubble Space Telescope (HST) Advanced Camera for Surveys images combined with the wide view of the Mosaic Camera on the National Science Foundation's 0.9-meter telescope at Kitt Peak National Observatory, part of the National Optical Astronomy Observatory, near Tucson, Ariz. Astronomers at the Space Telescope Science Institute (STScI) assembled the images into a mosaic. The mosaic was blended with a wider photograph taken by the Mosaic Camera.

These features are a forest of thousands of comet-like tentacles that are embedded along the inner rim of the nebula. The tentacles point toward the central star, which is a small but super-hot white dwarf (white dot in the center of the nebula) that seems to float in a sea of blue gas. These tentacles formed when a hot "stellar wind" of gas plowed into colder shells of dust and gas ejected previously by the doomed star.

These comet-like tentacles have been observed from ground-based telescopes for decades, but never have they been seen in such detail. They may actually lie in a disk encircling the hot star, like an animal's collar.

Imagination of Man

Space Flight ~ Soviet Union
(1957)

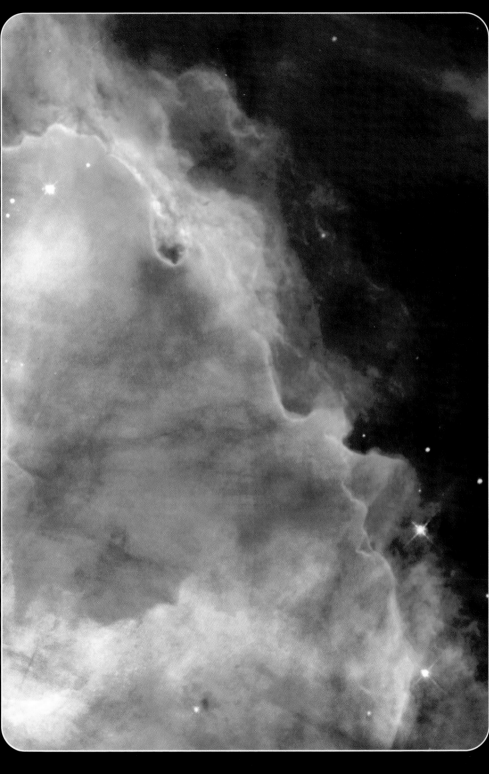

M17 (NGC 6618, Omega Nebula, Swan Nebula)

Resembling the fury of a raging sea, this image actually shows a bubbly ocean of glowing hydrogen gas and small amounts of other elements such as oxygen and sulfur.

The photograph, taken by NASA's Hubble Space Telescope, captures a small region within M17, a hotbed of star formation. M17, also known as the Omega or Swan Nebula, is located about 5,500 light-years away in the constellation Sagittarius. The image is being released to commemorate the thirteenth anniversary of Hubble's launch on April 24, 1990.

The wave-like patterns of gas have been sculpted and illuminated by a torrent of ultraviolet radiation from young massive stars, which lie outside the picture to the upper left. The glow of these patterns accentuates the three-dimensional structure of the gases. The ultraviolet radiation is carving and heating the surfaces of cold hydrogen gas clouds. The warmed surfaces glow orange and red in this photograph.

The intense heat and pressure cause some material to stream away from those surfaces, creating the glowing veil of even hotter greenish gas that masks background structures. The pressure on the tips of the waves may trigger new star formation within them.

The image, roughly three light-years across, was taken May 29-30, 1999, with the Wide Field Planetary Camera 2. The colors in the image represent various gases. Red represents sulfur; green, hydrogen; and blue, oxygen.

Imagination of Man

Personal Computer ~ Steve Jobs/Steve Wozniak
(1977)

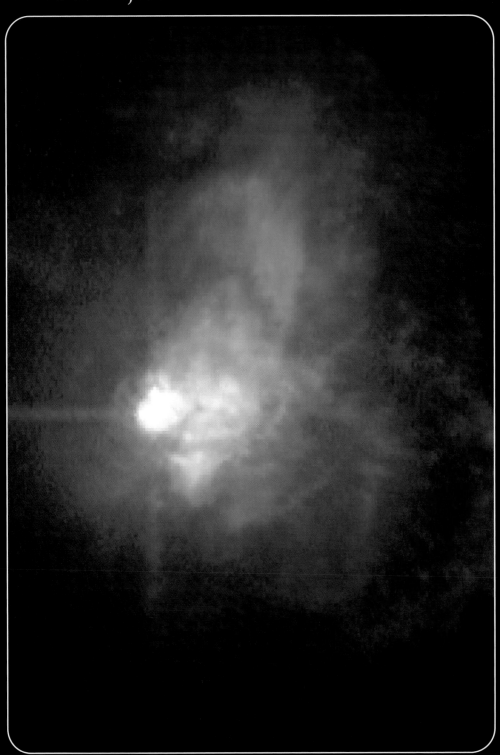

VY Canis Majoris

Using NASA's Hubble Space Telescope and the W.M. Keck Observatory in Kameula, Hawaii, astronomers have learned that the gaseous outflow from one of the brightest super-sized stars in the sky is more complex than originally thought.

The outbursts are from VY Canis Majoris, a red supergiant star that is also classified as a hypergiant because of its very high luminosity. The eruptions have formed loops, arcs, and knots of material moving at various speeds and in many different directions. The star has had many outbursts over the past 1,000 years as it nears the end of its life.

A team of astronomers at the University of Minnesota used NASA's Hubble Space Telescope and the W.M. Keck Observatory to measure the motions of the ejected material and to map the distribution of the highly polarized dust, which reflects light at a specific orientation. The polarized light shows how the dust is distributed. Astronomers combined the Hubble and Keck information to produce a three-dimensional image of the matter emitted from VY Canis Majoris.

Astronomers have studied VY Canis Majoris for more than a century. The star is located 5,000 light-years away. It is 500,000 times brighter and about thirty to forty times more massive than the Sun. If the Sun were replaced with the bloated VY Canis Majoris, its surface could extend to the orbit of Saturn.

Images with Hubble's Wide Field and Planetary Camera 2 revealed for the first time the complexity of the star's ejecta. The first images provided evidence that the brightest arcs and knots were created during several outbursts. The random orientations of the arcs also suggested that they were produced by localized eruptions from active regions on the star's surface.

The typical red supergiant phase lasts about 500,000 years. A massive star becomes a red supergiant near the end of its life, when it exhausts the hydrogen fuel at its core. As the core contracts under gravity, the outer layers expand, the star gets one hundred times larger, and it begins to lose mass at a higher rate. VY Canis Majoris has probably already shed about half of its mass, and it will eventually explode as a supernova.

Imagination of Man

Radar ~ Christian Hülsmeyer
(1904)

IMAGINATION SUPREME

Eagle Nebula, M16, NGC 6611

This eerie, dark structure, resembling an imaginary sea serpent's head, is a column of cool molecular hydrogen gas (two atoms of hydrogen in each molecule) and dust that is an incubator for new stars. The stars are embedded inside finger-like protrusions extending from the top of the nebula. Each "fingertip" is somewhat larger than our own solar system.

The pillar is slowly eroding away by the ultraviolet light from nearby hot stars, a process called "photoevaporation." As it does, small globules of especially dense gas buried within the cloud are uncovered. These globules have been dubbed "EGGs"—an acronym for "Evaporating Gaseous Globules." The shadows of the EGGs protect gas behind them, resulting in the finger-like structures at the top of the cloud.

Forming inside at least some of the EGGs are embryonic stars—stars that abruptly stop growing when the EGGs are uncovered and they are separated from the larger reservoir of gas from which they were drawing mass. Eventually the stars emerge, as the EGGs themselves succumb to photoevaporation.

The stellar EGGS are found, appropriately enough, in the "Eagle Nebula" (also called M16—the 16th object in Charles Messier's 18th century catalog of "fuzzy" permanent objects in the sky), a nearby star-forming region 6,500 light-years away in the constellation Serpens.

The picture was taken on April 1, 1995, with the Hubble Space Telescope Wide Field and Planetary Camera 2. The color image is constructed from three separate images taken in the light of emission from different types of atoms. Red shows emission from singly-ionized sulfur atoms. Green shows emission from hydrogen. Blue shows light emitted by doubly ionized oxygen atoms.

Imagination of Man

Theory of Relativity ~ Albert Einstein
(1909)

Crab Nebula NGC 1952 Cosmic Creation

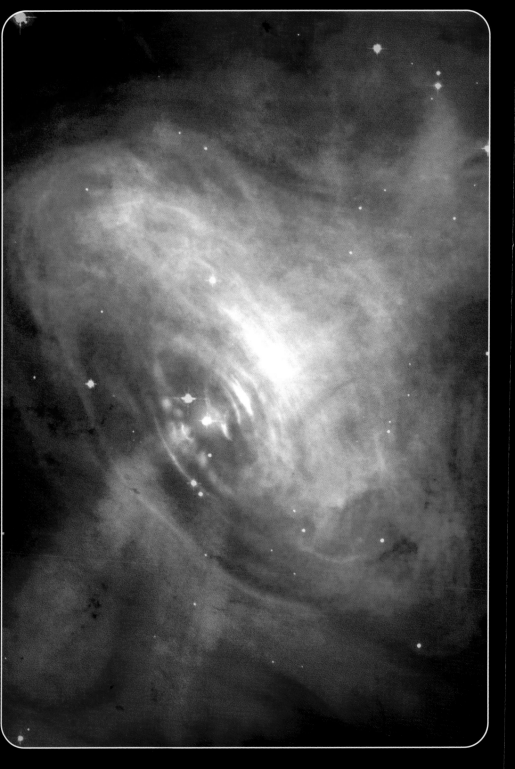

IMAGINATION SUPREME

Crab Nebula NGC 1952

Just when it seemed like the summer movie season had ended, two of NASA's Great Observatories have produced their own action movie. Multiple observations made over several months with NASA's Chandra X-Ray Observatory and the Hubble Space Telescope captured the spectacle of matter and antimatter propelled to near the speed of light by the Crab pulsar, a rapidly rotating neutron star the size of Manhattan. "Through this movie, the Crab Nebula has come to life," said Jeff Hester of Arizona State University in Tempe. He was lead author of a paper in the September 20, 2006 issue of *The Astrophysical Journal Letters*. "We can see how this awesome cosmic generator actually works," Mr. Hester said. The Crab was first observed by Chinese astronomers in AD 1054 and has since become one of the most studied objects in the sky. By combining the power of Chandra and Hubble, the movie reveals features never before seen in still images. By understanding the Crab, astronomers hope to unlock the secrets of how similar objects across the universe are powered.

Bright wisps can be seen moving outward at half the speed of light to form an expanding ring that is visible in both X-ray and optical images. These wisps appear to originate from a shock wave that shows up as an inner X-ray ring. This ring consists of about two dozen knots that form, brighten and fade, jitter around, and occasionally undergo outbursts that give rise to expanding clouds of particles, but remain in roughly the same location. "These data leave little doubt that the inner X-ray ring is the location of the shock wave that turns the high-speed wind from the pulsar into extremely energetic particles," reported Koji Mori, the paper's coauthor. He is from Penn State University, in University Park.

Another dramatic feature of the movie is a turbulent jet that lies perpendicular to the inner and outer rings. Violent internal motions are obvious, as is a slow motion outward into the surrounding nebula of particles and magnetic field. A third coauthor, David Burrows of Penn State, stated that, "The jet looks like steam from a high pressure boiler, except when you realize you are looking at a stream of matter and antimatter electrons moving at half the speed of light!" The inner region of the Crab Nebula around the pulsar was observed with Hubble on twenty-four occasions between August 2000 and April 2001 at eleven-day intervals, and with Chandra on eight occasions between November 2000 and April 2001. The Crab was observed with Chandra's Advanced CCD Imaging Spectrometer and Hubble's Wide Field Planetary Camera.

Neutron stars may "pulse" due to particle acceleration near the magnetic poles, which are not aligned with the rotation axis of the star. A newborn neutron star can **rotate 30 or more per times second***.*

Imagination of Man

Color Photography ~ James Clerk Maxwell (1861)

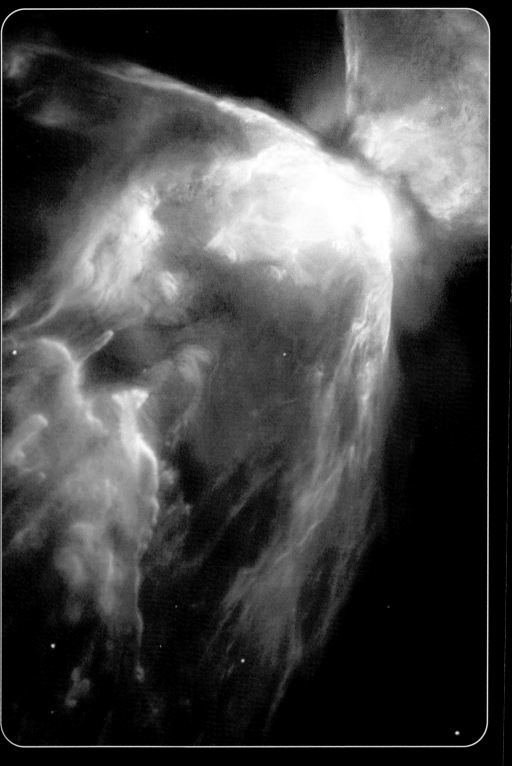

Bug Nebula NGC 6302

The Bug Nebula, NGC 6302, is one of the brightest and most extreme planetary nebulae known. The fiery dying star at its center is shrouded by a blanket of icy hailstones. This NASA Hubble Wide Field Camera 2 image shows impressive walls of compressed gas laced with trailing strands and bubbling outflows.

A dark, dusty torus surrounds the inner nebula (seen at the upper right). At the heart of the turmoil is one of the hottest stars known. Despite a sizzling temperature of at least 450,000 degrees Fahrenheit, the star itself has never been seen, as it is hidden by the blanket of dust and shines most brightly in the ultraviolet, making it hard to observe. The Bug Nebula lies about 4,000 light-years away in the southern constellation Scorpius.

Imagination of Man

Disposable Diapers ~ Marion Donovan
(1949)

Spiral Galaxy M74

Resembling festive lights on a holiday wreath, this NASA/ESA Hubble Space Telescope image of the nearby spiral galaxy M74 is an iconic reminder of the Christmas season. Bright knots of glowing gas light up the spiral arms, indicating a rich environment of star formation.

Messier 74, also called NGC 628, is a stunning example of a "grand-design" spiral galaxy that is viewed by Earth observers nearly face-on. Its perfectly symmetrical spiral arms emanate from the central nucleus and are dotted with clusters of young blue stars and glowing pink regions of ionized hydrogen (hydrogen atoms that have lost their electrons). These regions of star formation show an excess of light at ultraviolet wavelengths. Tracing along the spiral arms are winding dust lanes that also begin very near the galaxy's nucleus and follow along the length of the spiral arms.

M74 is located approximately thirty-two million light-years away in the direction of the constellation Pisces, the Fish. It is the dominant member of a small group of about half a dozen galaxies, the M74 galaxy group. In its entirety, it is estimated that M74 is home to about one hundred billion stars, making it slightly smaller than our Milky Way.

The spiral galaxy was first discovered by the French astronomer Pierre Méchain in 1780. Weeks later it was added to Charles Messier's famous catalog of deep-sky objects.

This Hubble image of M74 is a composite of Advanced Camera for Surveys data taken in 2003 and 2005. The filters used to create the color image isolate light from blue, visible, and infrared portions of the spectrum, as well as emission from ionized hydrogen (known as HII regions).

Imagination of Man

Barbie Doll ~ Ruth Handler
(1959)

Sombrero Galaxy M104

NASA's Hubble Space Telescope has trained its razor-sharp eye on one of the universe's most stately and photogenic galaxies, the Sombrero galaxy, Messier 104 (M104). The galaxy's hallmark is a brilliant-white bulbous core encircled by the thick dust lanes comprising the spiral structure of the galaxy. As seen from Earth, the galaxy is tilted nearly edge-on. We view it from just six degrees north of its equatorial plane. This brilliant galaxy was named the Sombrero because of its resemblance to the broad rim and high-topped Mexican hat.

At a relatively bright magnitude of plus eight, M104 is just beyond the limit of naked-eye visibility and is easily seen through small telescopes. The Sombrero lies at the southern edge of the rich Virgo cluster of galaxies and is one of the most massive objects in that group, equivalent to 800 billion suns. The galaxy is 50,000 light-years across and is located twenty-eight million light-years from Earth.

Hubble easily resolves M104's rich system of globular clusters, estimated to be nearly 2,000 in number—ten times as many as orbit our Milky Way galaxy. The ages of the clusters are similar to the clusters in the Milky Way, ranging from ten to thirteen billion years old. Embedded in the bright core of M104 is a smaller disk, which is tilted relative to the large disk. X-ray emission suggests that there is material falling into the compact core, where a one-billion-solar-mass black hole resides.

In the nineteenth century, some astronomers speculated that M104 was simply an edge-on disk of luminous gas surrounding a young star, which is prototypical of the genesis of our solar system. But in 1912, astronomer V. M. Slipher discovered that the hat-like object appeared to be rushing away from us at 700 miles per second. This enormous velocity offered some of the earliest clues that the Sombrero was really another galaxy, and that the universe was expanding in all directions.

The Hubble Heritage Team took these observations in May-June of 2003 with the space telescope's Advanced Camera for Surveys. Images were taken in three filters (red, green, and blue) to yield a natural-color image. The team took six pictures of the galaxy and then stitched them together to create the final composite image—one of the largest Hubble mosaics ever assembled.

Object Names: Sombrero Galaxy, M104, NGC 4594

Imagination of Man

Microprocessor ~ Ted Hoff, Jr.
(1971)

Globular Cluster NGC 6397

Looking like glittering jewels, the stars in this Hubble Space Telescope image at left are part of the ancient globular star cluster NGC 6397. Scattered among these brilliant stars are extremely faint stars. Hubble's Advanced Camera for Surveys has taken a census of the cluster stars, uncovering the faintest stars ever seen in a globular cluster. Globular clusters are spherical concentrations of hundreds of thousands of old stars.

The Advanced Camera found the faintest red dwarf stars (26th magnitude), which are cooler and much lower in mass than our Sun, and the dimmest white dwarfs (28th magnitude), the burned-out relics of normal stars. The light from the dimmest white dwarfs is equal to the light produced by a birthday candle on the Moon as seen from Earth.

The image at lower right shows the faintest red dwarf star (the red dot within the red circle) spied by Hubble.

The image at upper right pinpoints one of the dim white dwarfs (the blue dot within the blue circle) seen by Hubble. The white dwarf has been cooling for billions of years. It is so cool that instead of looking red, it has undergone a chemical change in its atmosphere that makes it appear blue.

The images were taken with visual and red filters. NGC 6397, one of the closest globular clusters to Earth, is 8,500 light-years away in the southern constellation Ara. The data for these images were obtained in March and April 2005.

Imagination of Man

Scotchgard ~ Patsy Sherman / Samuel Smith
(1952)

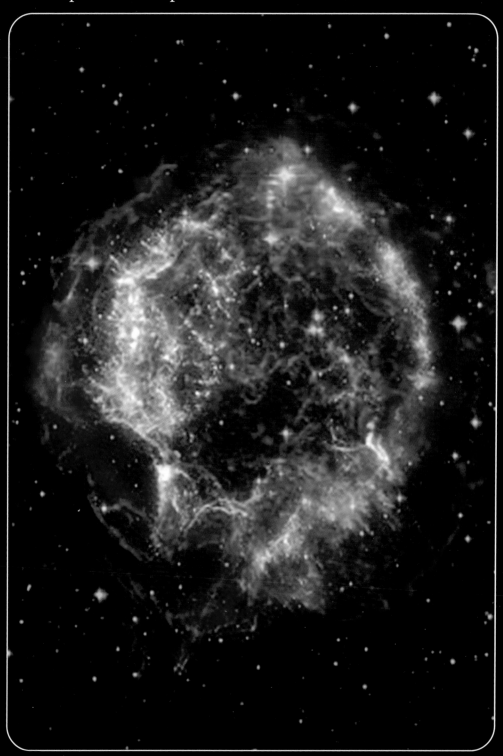

Cassiopeia A—Supernova Remnant

An enormous light echo etched in the sky by a fitful dead star was spotted by the infrared eyes of NASA's Spitzer Space Telescope. The surprising finding indicates that Cassiopeia A, the remnant of a star that died in a supernova explosion 325 years ago, is not resting peacefully. Instead, this dead star likely shot out at least one burst of energy as recently as fifty years ago.

"We had thought the stellar remains inside Cassiopeia A were just fading away," said a scientist from the University of Arizona, Tucson. "Spitzer came along and showed us this exploded star, one of the most intensively studied objects in the sky, is still undergoing death throes before heading to its final grave."

Infrared echoes trace the dusty journeys of light waves blasted away from supernova or erupting stars. As the light waves move outward, they heat up clumps of surrounding dust, causing them to glow in infrared light. The echo from Cassiopeia A is the first witnessed around a long-dead star and the largest ever seen. It was discovered by accident during a Spitzer instrument test.

A supernova remnant like Cassiopeia A typically consists of an outer shimmering shell of expelled material and a core skeleton of a once-massive star, called a neutron star. Neutron stars come in several varieties, ranging from intensely active to silent. Typically, a star that has recently died will continue to act up. Consequently, astronomers were puzzled that the star responsible for Cassiopeia A appeared to be silent so soon after its death.

The new infrared echo indicates the Cassiopeia A neutron star is active and may even be an exotic spastic type of object called a "magnetar." Magnetars are like screaming dead stars with eruptive surfaces that rupture and quake, pouring out tremendous amounts of high-energy gamma rays. Spitzer may have captured the "shriek" of such a star in the form of light zipping away through space and heating up its surroundings.

A close inspection of the Spitzer pictures revealed a blend of at least two light echoes around Cassiopeia A, one from its supernova explosion and one from the hiccup of activity that occurred around 1953. Additional Spitzer observations of these light echoes may help pin down their enigmatic source.

Imagination of Man

Electric Lighting ~Thomas Edison
(1879)

Rho Oph Star-Forming Region

Newborn stars peek out from beneath their natal blanket of dust in this dynamic image of the Rho Ophiuchi dark cloud from NASA's Spitzer Space Telescope.

Called "Rho Oph" by astronomers, it's one of the closest star-forming regions to our own solar system. Located near the constellations Scorpius and Ophiuchus, the nebula is about 407 light-years away from Earth.

Rho Oph is made up of a large main cloud of molecular hydrogen, a key molecule allowing new stars to form out of cold cosmic gas, with two long streamers trailing off in different directions. Recent studies using the latest X-ray and infrared observations reveal more than 300 young stellar objects within the large central cloud. Their median age is only 300,000 years, very young compared to some of the universe's oldest stars, which are more than 12 billion years old.

"Rho Oph is a favorite region for astronomers studying star formation. Because the stars are so young, we can observe them at a very early evolutionary stage, and because the Ophiuchus molecular cloud is relatively close, we can resolve more detail than in more distant clusters, like Orion," said the lead investigator of the new observations, from the Harvard-Smithsonian Center for Astrophysics in Cambridge, Massachusetts. This false-color image of Rho Oph's main cloud, Lynds 1688, was created with data from Spitzer's infrared array camera, which has the highest spatial resolution of Spitzer's three imaging instruments, and its multiband imaging photometer, best for detecting cooler materials.

The colors in this image reflect the relative temperatures and evolutionary states of the various stars. The youngest stars are surrounded by dusty disks of gas from which they and their potential planetary systems are forming. These young disk systems show up as red in this image. Some of these young stellar objects are surrounded by their own compact nebulae. More evolved stars, which have shed their natal material, are blue.

The extended white nebula in the center right of the image is a region of the cloud glowing in infrared light due to the heating of dust by bright young stars near the cloud's right edge. Fainter, multi-hued, diffuse emission fills the image. The color of the nebulosity depends on the temperature, composition, and size of the dust grains. Most of the stars forming now are concentrated in a filament of cold dense gas that shows up as a dark cloud in the lower center and left side of the image against the bright background of the warm dust.

Imagination of Man

Intelligible Telephone ~ Alexander Graham Bell
(1876)

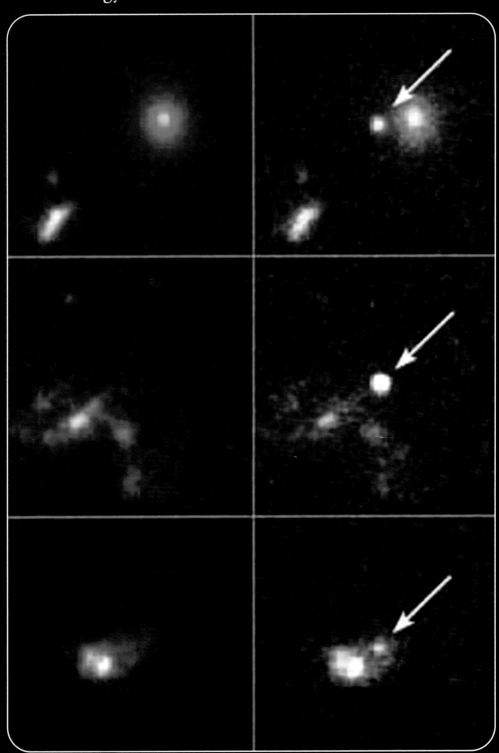

Dark Energy

These are images of three of the most distant supernovae known, discovered using the Hubble Space Telescope as a supernova search engine. The stars exploded back when the universe was approximately half its current age. The light is just arriving at Earth now. Supernovae are so bright they can be seen far away and far back in time. This allows astronomers to trace the expansion rate of the universe, and to determine how it is affected by the repulsive push of dark energy, an unknown form of energy that pervaded space.

WHAT IS DARK ENERGY?

Dark energy is an unknown form of energy that radiates from deep space. It behaves in the opposite manner from gravity. Rather than pulling galaxies together it pushes them apart.

DID ANYONE PREDICT DARK ENERGY?

Dark energy is a complete surprise. However, Albert Einstein theorized the existence of a repulsive form of gravity in space that would balance the universe against normal gravity and keep it from imploding. Einstein called it the "cosmological constant."

HOW DOES DARK ENERGY AFFECT THE UNIVERSE?

Dark energy makes up the bulk of the universe's mass/energy budget. If dark energy is stable the universe will continue expanding and accelerating forever. If dark energy is unstable the universe could ultimately come unglued to the point where stars, planets, and even atoms come apart, a doomsday scenario called the "big rip." Dark energy might also flip such that it becomes an attractive force and causes the universe to implode in a "big crunch."

HOW CAN HUBBLE "SEE" DARK ENERGY?

Hubble can measure the faint glow of distant supernovae, stars that exploded billions of years ago. Supernovae trace the expansion history of the universe, hence, how dark energy "pushed" on space over the past epochs. Every second a star explodes somewhere in the universe, so it's a matter of Hubble looking in the right place at the right time.

DOES HUBBLE PROVE HOW DARK ENERGY REALLY BEHAVES?

These latest Hubble observations show that dark energy is not changing its behavior over time, and so may be the "constant" Einstein predicted. However, more observations are needed over the coming decade.

Imagination of Man

Practical Typewriter ~ Christopher Sholes / Carlos Glidden
(1867)

Warped Edge-On Galaxy ESO 510-G13

NASA's Hubble Space Telescope has captured an image of an unusual edge-on galaxy, revealing remarkable details of its warped dusty disk and showing how colliding galaxies spawn the formation of new generations of stars.

The dust and spiral arms of normal spiral galaxies, like our own Milky Way, appear flat when viewed edge-on. This month's Hubble Heritage image of ESO 510-G13 shows a galaxy that, by contrast, has an unusual twisted disk structure, first seen in ground-based photographs obtained at the European Southern Observatory (ESO) in Chile. ESO 510-G13 lies in the southern constellation Hydra, roughly 150 million light-years from Earth.

Details of the structure of ESO 510-G13 are visible because the interstellar dust clouds that trace its disk are silhouetted from behind by light from the galaxy's bright, smooth, central bulge.

The strong warping of the disk indicates that ESO 510-G13 has recently undergone a collision with a nearby galaxy and is in the process of swallowing it. Gravitational forces distort the structures of the galaxies as their stars, gas, and dust merge together in a process that takes millions of years. Eventually the disturbances will die out, and ESO 510-G13 will become a normal-appearing single galaxy.

In the outer regions of ESO 510-G13, especially on the right-hand side of the image, we see that the twisted disk contains not only dark dust, but also bright clouds of blue stars. This shows that hot young stars are being formed in the disk. Astronomers believe that the formation of new stars may be triggered by collisions between galaxies as their interstellar clouds smash together and are compressed.

Imagination of Man

Practical Electric Motor ~ William Sturgeon
(1832)

IMAGINATION SUPREME

Monocerotis Light Echo V838

Starry Night, Vincent van Gogh's famous painting, is renowned for its bold whorls of light sweeping across a raging night sky. Although this image of the heavens came only from the artist's restless imagination, a new picture from NASA's Hubble Space Telescope bears remarkable similarities to the van Gogh work, complete with never-before-seen spirals of dust swirling across trillions of miles of interstellar space. This image, obtained with the Advanced Camera for Surveys on February 8, 2004, is Hubble's latest view of an expanding halo of light around a distant star, named V838 Monocerotis (V838 Mon). The illumination of interstellar dust comes from the red supergiant star at the middle of the image, which gave off a flashbulb-like pulse of light two years ago. V838 Mon is located about 20,000 light-years away from Earth in the direction of the constellation Monoceros, placing the star at the outer edge of our Milky Way galaxy.

Called a "light echo," the expanding illumination of a dusty cloud around the star has been revealing remarkable structures ever since the star suddenly brightened for several weeks in early 2002. Though Hubble has followed the light echo in several snapshots, this new image shows swirls, or eddies, in the dusty cloud for the first time. These eddies are probably caused by turbulence in the dust and gas around the star as they slowly expand away. The dust and gas were likely ejected from the star in a previous explosion, similar to the 2002 event, which occurred some tens of thousands of years ago. The surrounding dust remained invisible and unsuspected until suddenly illuminated by the brilliant explosion of the central star two years ago.

The Hubble telescope has imaged V838 Mon and its light echo several times since the star's outburst in January 2002, in order to follow the constantly changing appearance of the dust as the pulse of illumination continues to expand away from the star at the speed of light. During the outburst event, the normally faint star suddenly brightened, becoming 600,000 times more luminous than our Sun. It was thus one of the brightest stars in the entire Milky Way, until it faded away again in April 2002. The star has some similarities to a class of objects called "novae," which suddenly increase in brightness due to thermonuclear explosions at their surfaces; however, the detailed behavior of V838 Mon, in particular its extremely red color, has been completely different from any previously known nova. Nature's own piece of performance art, this structure will continue to change its appearance in coming years as the light from the stellar outburst continues to propagate outward and bounce off more distant black clouds of dust. Astronomers expect the echoes to remain visible for at least the rest of the current decade.

Imagination of Man

Electrical Telegraph ~ Samuel F. B. Morse
(1837)

Jupiter

The most massive planet in our solar system, with four planet-sized moons and many smaller moons, Jupiter forms a kind of miniature solar system. Jupiter resembles a star in composition. In fact, if it had been about eighty times more massive, it would have become a star rather than a planet.

On January 7, 1610, using his primitive telescope, astronomer Galileo Galilei saw four small "stars" near Jupiter. He had discovered Jupiter's four largest moons, now called *Io, Europa, Ganymede,* and *Callisto.* Collectively, these four moons are known today as the Galilean satellites.

Galileo would be astonished at what we have learned about Jupiter and its moons in the past thirty years. Io is the most volcanically active body in our solar system. Ganymede is the largest planetary moon and is the only moon in the solar system known to have its own magnetic field. A liquid ocean may lie beneath the frozen crust of Europa. Icy oceans may also lie deep beneath the crusts of Callisto and Ganymede. In 2003 alone, astronomers discovered twenty-three new moons orbiting the giant planet, giving Jupiter a total moon count of forty-nine officially named—the most in the solar system. The numerous small outer moons may be asteroids captured by the giant planet's gravity. Jupiter's appearance is a tapestry of beautiful colors and atmospheric features. Most visible clouds are composed of ammonia. Water exists deep below and can sometimes be seen through clear spots in the clouds. The planet's "stripes" are dark belts and light zones created by strong east-west winds in Jupiter's upper atmosphere. Within these belts and zones are storm systems that have raged for years. The Great Red Spot, a giant spinning storm, has been observed for more than 300 years.

The composition of Jupiter's atmosphere is similar to that of the Sun—mostly hydrogen and helium. Deep in the atmosphere, the pressure and temperature increase, compressing the hydrogen gas into a liquid. At depths about a third of the way down, the hydrogen becomes metallic and electrically conducting. In this metallic layer, Jupiter's powerful magnetic field is generated by electrical currents driven by Jupiter's fast rotation. At the center, the immense pressure may support a solid core of ice-rock about the size of Earth. Jupiter's enormous magnetic field is nearly 20,000 times as powerful as the Earth's. Trapped within Jupiter's magnetosphere (the area in which magnetic field lines encircle the planet from pole to pole) are swarms of charged particles. Jupiter's rings and moons are embedded in an intense radiation belt of electrons and ions trapped in the magnetic field.

Imagination of Man

Father of Modern Observational Astronomy ~ Galileo
(1564-1692)

Saturn

Saturn was the most distant of the five planets known to the ancients. In 1610, Italian astronomer Galileo Galilei was the first to gaze at Saturn through a telescope. To his surprise, he saw a pair of objects on either side of the planet. He sketched them as separate spheres and wrote that Saturn appeared to be triple-bodied. Continuing his observations over the next few years, Galileo drew the lateral bodies as arms or handles attached to Saturn. In 1659, Dutch astronomer Christiaan Huygens, using a more powerful telescope than Galileo's, proposed that Saturn was surrounded by a thin flat ring. In 1675, Italian-born astronomer Jean-Dominique Cassini discovered a "division" between what are now called the A and B rings. It is now known that the gravitational influence of Saturn's moon Mimas is responsible for the Cassini Division, which is 4,800 kilometers (3,000 miles) wide.

Like Jupiter, Saturn is made mostly of hydrogen and helium. Its volume is 755 times greater than that of Earth. Winds in the upper atmosphere reach 500 meters (1,600 feet) per second in the equatorial region. (In contrast, the strongest hurricane-force winds on Earth top out at about 110 meters, or 360 feet, per second.) These super-fast winds, combined with heat rising from within the planet's interior, cause the yellow and gold bands visible in the atmosphere.

Saturn's ring system is the most extensive and complex in the solar system, extending hundreds of thousands of kilometers from the planet. In the early 1980s, NASA's two Voyager spacecraft revealed that Saturn's rings are made mostly of water ice, and they found "braided" rings, ringlets, and "spokes"—dark features in the rings that circle the planet at different rates from that of the surrounding ring material. Material in the rings ranges in size from a few micrometers to several tens of meters. Two of Saturn's small moons orbit within gaps in the main rings.

Saturn has fifty-two known natural satellites (moons) and there are probably many more waiting to be discovered. Saturn's largest satellite, Titan, is a bit bigger than the planet Mercury. (Titan is the second-largest moon in the solar system; only Jupiter's moon Ganymede is bigger.) Titan is shrouded in a thick nitrogen-rich atmosphere that might be similar to what Earth's was like long ago.

Imagination of Man

Electric Battery ~ Alessandro Volta
(1799)

Cosmic Collisions Galore!

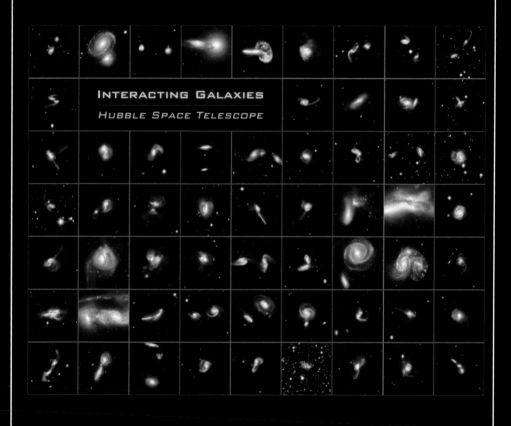

INTERACTING GALAXIES

HUBBLE SPACE TELESCOPE

Cosmic Collisions Galore!

Astronomy textbooks typically present galaxies as staid, solitary, and majestic island worlds of glittering stars.

But galaxies have a dynamical side. They have close encounters that sometimes end in grand mergers and overflowing sites of new star birth as the **colliding galaxies morph into wondrous new shapes**.

Today, in celebration of the Hubble Space Telescope's 18th launch anniversary, fifty-nine views of colliding galaxies constitute the largest collection of Hubble images ever released to the public. This new Hubble atlas dramatically illustrates how galaxy collisions produce a remarkable variety of intricate structures in never-before-seen detail.

Astronomers observe only one out of a million galaxies in the nearby universe in the act of colliding. However, galaxy mergers were much more common long ago when they were closer together, because the expanding universe was smaller. Astronomers study how gravity choreographs their motions in the game of celestial bumper cars and try to observe them in action.

For all their violence, galactic smash-ups take place at a glacial rate by human standards—timescales on the order of several hundred million years. The images in the Hubble atlas capture snapshots of the various merging galaxies at various stages in their collision.

Most of the fifty-nine new Hubble images are part of a large investigation of luminous and ultra-luminous infrared galaxies called the GOALS project (Great Observatories All-sky LIRG Survey). This survey combines observations from Hubble, NASA's Spitzer Space Telescope, NASA's Chandra X-ray Observatory, and NASA's Galaxy Evolution Explorer. The majority of the Hubble observations are led by Aaron S. Evans of the University of Virginia, Charlottesville, the National Radio Astronomy Observatory, and Stony Brook University.

Imagination of Man

Steam Locomotive ~ Richard Trevithick
(1802)

Helix Nebula NGC 7293

A bunch of rowdy comets are colliding and kicking up dust around a dead star, according to new observations from NASA's Spitzer Space Telescope. The dead star lies at the center of the much-photographed Helix nebula, a shimmering cloud of gas with an eerie resemblance to a giant eye. "We were surprised to see so much dust around this star," said a doctor at the University of Arizona, Tucson, and lead author of a paper on the results appearing in the March 1 issue of *Astrophysical Journal Letters*. "The dust must be coming from comets that survived the death of their sun."

Spitzer's spectacular new view of the Helix nebula shows colors as seen in infrared. The dusty dead star appears as a dot in the middle of the nebula, like a red pupil in a green monster's eye. The Helix nebula, located about 700 light-years away in the constellation Aquarius, was formed when a star much like our Sun died and sloughed off its skin, or outer layers. Radiation from the dead star's hot core, called a "white dwarf," heats the expelled material, causing it to fluoresce with vivid colors. This cosmic beauty, termed a "planetary nebula," won't last long. In about 10,000 years, its shiny clouds will fade, leaving the white dwarf and its circling comets to cool down alone in empty space.

Astronomers have long studied the white dwarf at the center of the Helix nebula, but nobody had detected any dust close to it until now. Spitzer, an infrared space-based observatory, was able to pick up the glow of a dusty disk circling around the stellar corpse at a distance of about 35 to 150 astronomical units (an astronomical unit is the distance between our Sun and Earth, which is 150 million kilometers or 93 million miles).

At first, the astronomers were shocked to see the dust. They said that when the star died, expelling its outer layers, dust in the system should have been blown away. The team then obtained more detailed data, which again pointed to the presence of a dusty disk. Where is the dust coming from? According to the astronomers, it is most likely being freshly churned up by comets smashing into each other in the outer fringes of the white dwarf's system. A few million years ago, before the white dwarf formed, when it was still a lively star like our Sun, its comets and possibly planets would have been in stable orbits, harmoniously traveling around the star. But when the star died, any inner planets would have burned up or been swallowed as the star expanded. Outer planets, asteroids, and comets would have been jostled about and thrown into each other's paths.

Imagination of Man

Safety Match ~ Carl Lundstrom
(1845)

Galaxy Centaurus A

A dramatic new Chandra image of the nearby galaxy Centaurus A provides one of the best views to date of the effects of an active supermassive black hole. Opposing jets of high-energy particles can be seen extending to the outer reaches of the galaxy, and numerous smaller black holes in binary star systems are also visible. The image was made from an ultra-deep look at the galaxy Centaurus A, equivalent to more than seven days of continuous observations. Centaurus A is the nearest galaxy to Earth thta contains a supermassive black hole actively powering a jet. A prominent X-ray jet extending for 13,000 light-years points to the upper left in the image, with a shorter "counterjet" aimed in the opposite direction. Astronomers think that such jets are important vehicles for transporting energy from the black hole to the much larger dimensions of a galaxy, and affecting the rate at which stars form there. High-energy electrons spiraling around magnetic field lines produce the X-ray emission from the jet and counterjet. This emission quickly saps the energy from the electrons, so they must be continually reaccelerated or the X-rays will fade out. Knot-like features in the jets detected in the Chandra image show where the acceleration of particles to high energies is currently occurring, and provides important clues to understanding the process that accelerates the electrons to near-light speeds.

The inner part of the X-ray jet close to the black hole is dominated by these knots of X-ray emission, which probably come from shock waves—akin to sonic booms—caused by the jet. Farther from the black hole there is more diffuse X-ray emission in the jet. The cause of particle acceleration in this part of the jet is unknown. Hundreds of point-like sources are also seen in the Chandra image. Many of these are X-ray binaries that contain a stellar-mass black hole and a companion star in orbit around one another. Determining the population and properties of these black holes should help scientists better understand the evolution of massive stars and the formation of black holes.

Another surprise was the detection of two particularly bright X-ray binaries. These sources may contain stellar mass black holes that are unusually massive, and this Chandra observation might have caught them gobbling up material at a high rate.

In this image, low-energy X-rays are colored red, intermediate-energy X-rays are green, and the highest-energy X-rays detected by Chandra are blue. The dark-green and blue bands running almost perpendicular to the jet are dust lanes that absorb X-rays. This dust lane was created when Centaurus A merged with another galaxy perhaps 100 million years ago.

Imagination of Man

Microscope ~ Hans and Zacharias Janssen
(1590)

Menzel 3, The "Ant Nebula"

From ground-based telescopes, the so-called "ant nebula" (Menzel 3, or Mz 3) resembles the head and thorax of a garden-variety ant. This dramatic NASA/ESA Hubble Space Telescope image, showing ten times more detail, reveals the "ant's" body as a pair of fiery lobes protruding from a dying Sun-like star. The Hubble images directly challenge old ideas about the last stages in the lives of stars. By observing Sun-like stars as they approach their deaths, the Hubble Heritage image of Mz 3—along with pictures of other planetary nebulae—shows that our Sun's fate probably will be more interesting, complex, and striking than astronomers imagined just a few years ago.

Though approaching the violence of an explosion, the ejection of gas from the dying star at the center of Mz 3 has intriguing symmetrical patterns unlike the chaotic patterns expected from an ordinary explosion. Scientists using Hubble would like to understand how a spherical star can produce such prominent non-spherical symmetries in the gas that it ejects. One possibility is that the central star of Mz 3 has a closely orbiting companion that exerts strong gravitational tidal forces, which shape the out-flowing gas. For this to work, the orbiting companion star would have to be close to the dying star, about the distance of the Earth from the Sun. At that distance the orbiting companion star wouldn't be far outside the hugely bloated hulk of the dying star. It's even possible that the dying star has consumed its companion, which now orbits inside of it, much like the duck in the wolf's belly in the story "Peter and the Wolf."

A second possibility is that, as the dying star spins, its strong magnetic fields are wound up into complex shapes like spaghetti in an eggbeater. Charged winds moving at speeds up to 1000 kilometers per second from the star, much like those in our Sun's solar wind but millions of times denser, are able to follow the twisted field lines on their way out into space. These dense winds can be rendered visible by ultraviolet light from the hot central star or from highly supersonic collisions with the ambient gas that excites the material into florescence.

No other planetary nebula observed by Hubble resembles Mz 3 very closely. M2-9 comes close, but the outflow speeds in Mz 3 are up to ten times larger than those of M2-9. Interestingly, the very massive young star, Eta Carinae, shows a very similar outflow pattern.

Imagination of Man

Piano ~ Bartolomeo Cristofori
(1655-1731)

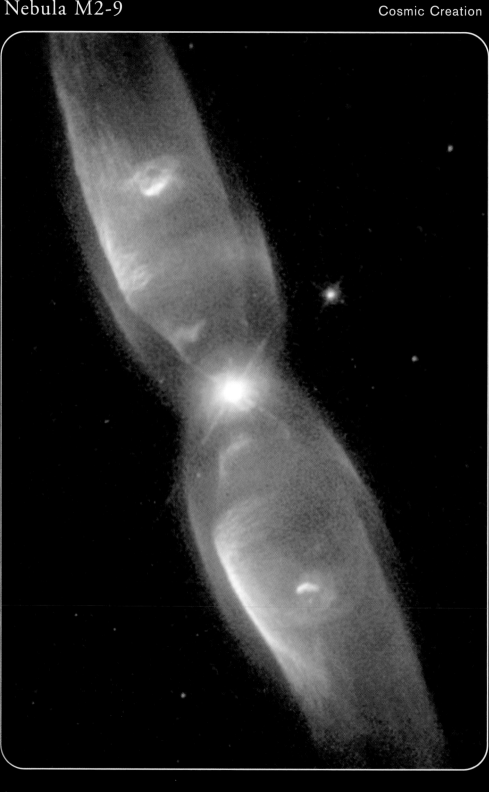

Nebula M2-9

M2-9 is a striking example of a "butterfly" or a bipolar planetary nebula. Another more revealing name might be the "Twin Jet Nebula." If the nebula is sliced across the star, each side of it appears much like a pair of exhausts from jet engines. Indeed, because of the nebula's shape and the measured velocity of the gas, in excess of 200 miles per second, astronomers believe that the description as a super-super-sonic jet exhaust is quite apt. Ground-based studies have shown that the nebula's size increases with time, suggesting that the stellar outburst that formed the lobes occurred just 1,200 years ago.

The central star in M2-9 is known to be one of a very close pair which orbit one another at perilously close distances. It is even possible that one star is being engulfed by the other. Astronomers suspect the gravity of one star pulls weakly bound gas from the surface of the other and flings it into a thin dense disk which surrounds both stars and extends well into space.

The disk can actually be seen in shorter exposure images obtained with the Hubble telescope. It measures approximately ten times the diameter of Pluto's orbit. Models of the type that are used to design jet engines ("hydrodynamics") show that such a disk can successfully account for the jet-exhaust-like appearance of M2-9. The high-speed wind from one of the stars rams into the surrounding disk, which serves as a nozzle. The wind is deflected in a perpendicular direction and forms the pair of jets that we see in the nebula's image.

This is much the same process that takes place in a jet engine: The burning and expanding gases are deflected by the engine walls through a nozzle to form long collimated jets of hot air at high speeds.

M2-9 is 2,100 light-years away in the constellation Ophiucus. The observation was taken August 2, 1997, by the Hubble telescope's Wide Field and Planetary Camera 2. In this image, neutral oxygen is shown in red, once-ionized nitrogen in green, and twice-ionized oxygen in blue.

Imagination of Man

Electric Vacuum Cleaner ~ Hubert Cecil Booth
(1901)

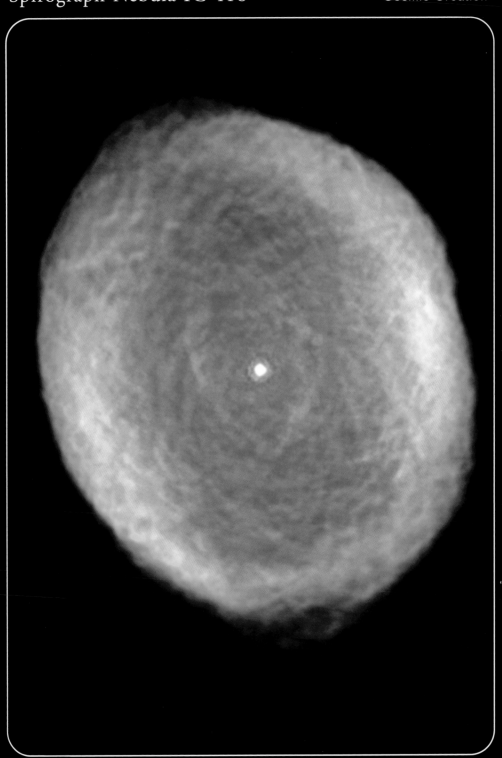

Spirograph Nebula IC 418

Glowing like a multi-faceted jewel, the planetary nebula IC 418 lies about 2,000 light-years from Earth in the direction of the constellation Lepus. This photograph is one of the latest from NASA's Hubble Space Telescope, obtained with the Wide Field Planetary Camera 2.

A planetary nebula represents the final stage in the evolution of a star similar to our Sun. The star at the center of IC 418 was a red giant a few thousand years ago, but then ejected its outer layers into space to form the nebula, which has now expanded to a diameter of about 0.1 light-year. The stellar remnant at the center is the hot core of the red giant, from which ultraviolet radiation floods out into the surrounding gas, causing it to fluoresce. Over the next several thousand years, the nebula will gradually disperse into space, and then the star will cool and fade away for billions of years as a white dwarf. Our own Sun is expected to undergo a similar fate, but fortunately this will not occur until some 5 billion years from now.

The Hubble image of IC 418 is shown in a false-color representation, based on Wide Field Planetary Camera 2 exposures taken in February and September 1999 through filters that isolate light from various chemical elements. Red shows emission from ionized nitrogen (the coolest gas in the nebula, located furthest from the hot nucleus), green shows emission from hydrogen, and blue traces the emission from ionized oxygen (the hottest gas, closest to the central star). The remarkable textures seen in the nebula are newly revealed by the Hubble telescope, and their origin is still uncertain.

Imagination of Man

Jet Propulsion ~ Hans Joachim Pabst von Ohain
(1936)

Bow Shock Near Young Star LL Ori

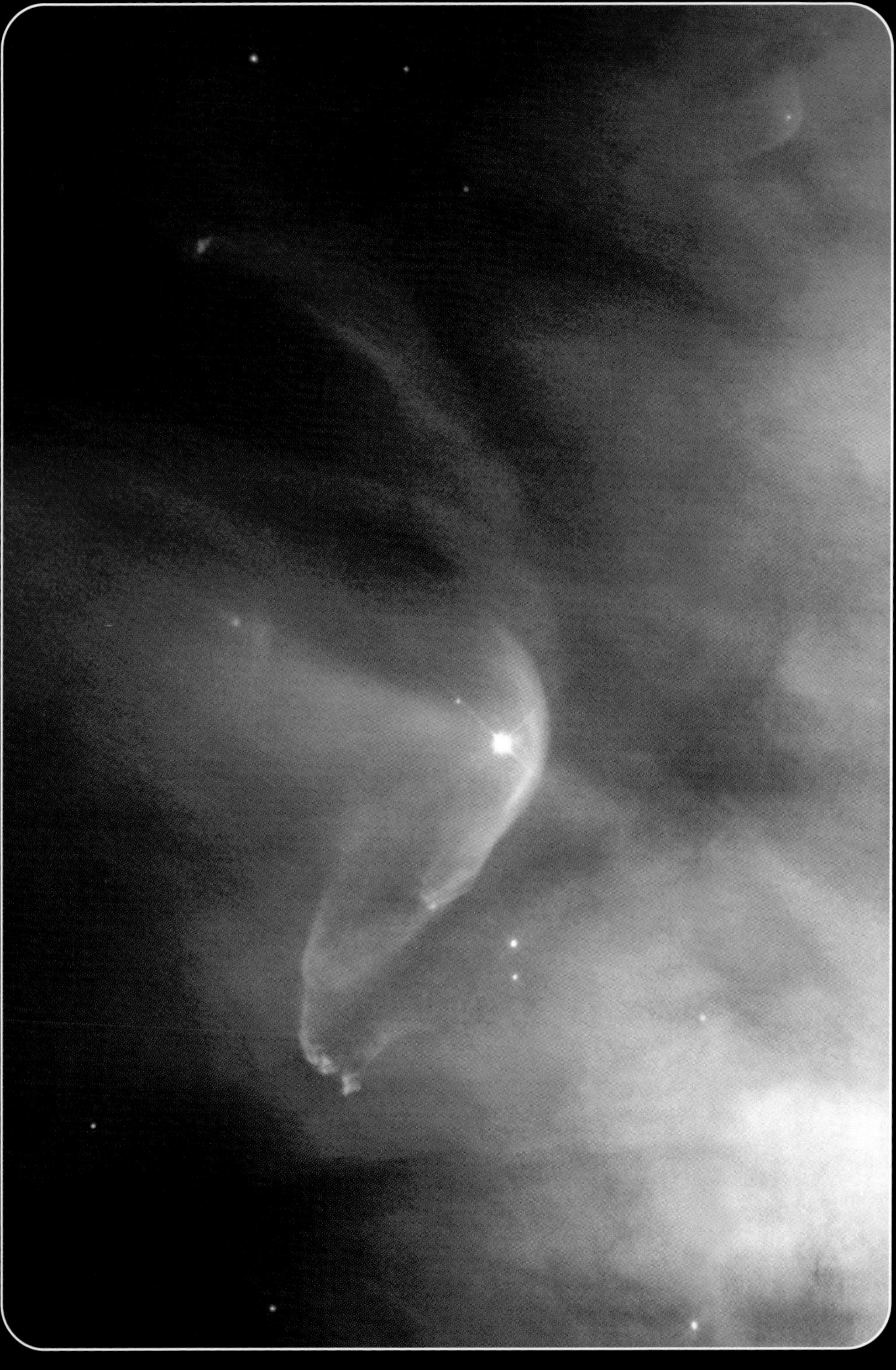

Bow Shock Near Young Star LL Ori

NASA's Hubble Space Telescope continues to reveal various stunning and intricate treasures that reside within the nearby, intense, star-forming region known as the Great Nebula in Orion. One such jewel is the bow shock around the very young star, LL Ori, featured in this Hubble Heritage image.

Named for the crescent-shaped wave made by a ship as it moves through water, a bow shock can be created in space when two streams of gas collide. LL Ori emits a vigorous solar wind, a stream of charged particles moving rapidly outward from the star. Our own Sun has a less energetic version of this wind that is responsible for auroral displays on the Earth.

The material in the fast wind from LL Ori collides with slow-moving gas evaporating away from the center of the Orion Nebula, which is located to the lower right in this Heritage image. The surface where the two winds collide is the crescent-shaped bow shock seen in the image.

Unlike a water wave made by a ship, this interstellar bow shock is a three-dimensional structure. The filamentary emission has a very distinct boundary on the side facing away from LL Ori, but is diffuse on the side closest to the star, a characteristic common to many bow shocks.

A second, fainter bow shock can be seen around a star near the upper right-hand corner of the Heritage image. Astronomers have identified numerous shock fronts in this complex star-forming region and are using this data to understand the many complex phenomena associated with the birth of stars.

This image was taken in February 1995 as part of the Hubble Orion Nebula mosaic. A close visitor in our Milky Way galaxy, the nebula is only 1,500 light-years from Earth. The filters used in this color composite represent oxygen, nitrogen, and hydrogen emissions.

Imagination of Man

Penicillin ~ Sir Alexander Fleming
(1928)

Hubble Ultra Deep Field

Galaxies, galaxies everywhere—as far as NASA's Hubble Space Telescope can see. This view of nearly 10,000 galaxies is the deepest visible-light image of the cosmos. Called the Hubble Ultra Deep Field, this galaxy-studded view represents a "deep" core sample of the universe, cutting across billions of light-years.

The snapshot includes galaxies of various ages, sizes, shapes, and colors. The smallest, reddest galaxies, about 100, may be among the most distant known, existing when the universe was just 800 million years old. The nearest galaxies—the larger, brighter, well-defined spirals and ellipticals—thrived about one billion years ago, when the cosmos was 13 billion years old.

In vibrant contrast to the rich harvest of classic spiral and elliptical galaxies, there is a zoo of oddball galaxies littering the field. Some look like toothpicks; others like links on a bracelet. A few appear to be interacting. These oddball galaxies chronicle a period when the universe was younger and more chaotic. Order and structure were just beginning to emerge.

The Ultra Deep Field observations, taken by the Advanced Camera for Surveys, represent a narrow, deep view of the cosmos. Peering into the Ultra Deep Field is like looking through an eight-foot-long soda straw.

In ground-based photographs, the patch of sky in which the galaxies reside (just one-tenth the diameter of the full Moon) is largely empty. Located in the constellation Fornax, the region is so empty that only a handful of stars within the Milky Way galaxy can be seen in the image.

In this image, blue and green correspond to colors that can be seen by the human eye, such as hot, young, blue stars and the glow of Sun-like stars in the disks of galaxies. Red represents near-infrared light, which is invisible to the human eye, such as the red glow of dust-enshrouded galaxies.

The image required 800 exposures taken over the course of 400 Hubble orbits around Earth. The total amount of exposure time was 11.3 days, taken between September 24, 2003, and January 16, 2004.

Imagination of Man

Hubble Space Telescope ~ NASA
(1990)

HEAVENLY CREATIONS ON CANVAS

The beautiful live images in this Heavenly Creations Gallery have been enlarged and reproduced onto canvas to decorate your home or office as Inspiring Heavenly Art. Each piece is breathtaking and represents live Heavenly bodies in the Heavens above. On the following page are a few of the most popular images that are available in two sizes, and can be ordered online.

These Giclée prints have been enlarged up to 400-500 percent from their original print size and allow you to see much more detail in many of the images, such as dozens of spiral galaxies that appear only as small dots of light on the original prints. Each print is available in two sizes, up to forty inches, and come with a document explaining the image.

Each of these Giclée prints has a lifespan of up to 120 years without any visible signs of fading, and come with a thirty-day money-back guarantee.

If you are not awe inspired and 100 percent satisfied with your Giclée print when you receive it, you can return it in its original condition and receive a full refund. These beautiful works of celestial art will not only beatify your home and inspire you, but can be used as gifts to inspire your friends and family.

To view additional images and to purchase these canvases go to: http://www.TheSecretDoorway.com or call 1-800-622-4820.

Infrared Eagle Nebula

V838 Monocerotis Light Echo

Cone Nebula NGC 2264

Helix Nebula

Small Magellanic Cloud NGC 602

Crab Nebula NGC 1952

Veil Nebula—Segment #1

Veil Nebula—Segment #2

Veil Nebula—Segment #3

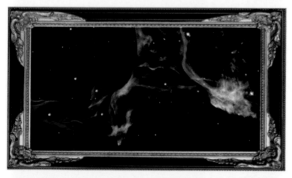

Sombrero Galaxy

ACKNOWLEDGMENTS

I WOULD LIKE TO THANK NASA AND THE ASSOCIATED ORGANIZATIONS MENtioned in the credits section of this book that are responsible for the Hubble, Spitzer, and other telescopes. None of these photos would be available without their hard work and dedication.

Thank you to everyone who wrote background information on these findings from Hubble and Spitzer, to help us better understand how this grand universe is unfolding before us. The world is grateful to all the men and women who have dedicated their lives to bring into view the Grandest Drama of all time, some even at the risk of their own lives. You are performing a valuable service for a noble cause to *"Look up into the heavens"* and see *"Who created all the stars?"*

I would like to acknowledge Mary Jo Zazueta of To The Point Solutions for her skillful work on the interior design; and David Yanor for his work on the glossary.

Thanks also to Zoom Astronomy at Enchanted Learning, and the good folks at CalTech.

Finally, and most importantly, I thank my wife, Diane, for her love and patience during this project and my daughters, Crystal, Tara, and Megan, for their love and for just being themselves. You all mean the world to me.

Also, I want to thank my sisters, Rose Mary, Rita, and Renee, for their helpful input and encouragement; and thank you to my friends who read the manuscript and gave me feedback.

ABOUT THE AUTHOR

After the death of his father, and with his mother working full-time to support the family, Paul Hutchins lacked direction and guidance in his life. As a young teenager he became involved in a life of crime and drugs. One day, he found himself in a high-speed car chase being shot at by the local sheriff as he and his friend ducked their heads and swerved their car back and forth so as not to get hit by the flying bullets.

At the age of nineteen, after considering suicide, the author had a life-changing experience that turned him around and saved his life. This experience kept him from going to prison with his brother, who was later shot in the head and killed; and his friend, who was featured on America's Most Wanted for murder and who was later captured.

It is now Hutchin's goal, through writing, to help others who may have lost direction and hopefully provide some guidance in their lives; to pause for a moment, and take a look around at what they are doing with their lives and ask: How could my life be different? What good could I be doing? And, what difference could I make, if I just used my gift of creative imagination?

The author originally set out to write about the imagination of man and how it is the force that shapes the world around us. Upon asking himself, What is the greatest example of imagination he could think of; his first thought was the design of the universe. He had remembered seeing a couple of photos from the Hubble Space Telescope, and did a Google search that came across the Hubble website.

Upon seeing the Hubble image of the Sombrero Galaxy for the first time, he knew immediately he had to change his subject from the imagination of man to the Supreme Imagination behind the design of the universe. (The Sombrero Galaxy is a famous galaxy photographed by NASA's Hubble telescope, bulging in the center from 800 billion stars.) Being familiar with a profound passage from the book of Isaiah he felt compelled to publish the link between the unimaginable energy source behind the design of the universe and this very curious invitation recorded 2,700 years ago in the book of Isaiah where it reads: *"Look up into the heavens. Who created all the stars? He brings them out like an army, one after another, calling each by its name. Because of his great power and incomparable strength, not a single one is missing."*

GLOSSARY

Andromeda Galaxy: This is a major spiral galaxy, 2.2 million light-years from Earth. Gravitationally bound to the Milky Way galaxy with which it shares membership in the Local Group.

Antennae Galaxies (NGC 4038-4039): A merging pair of galaxies. A famous pair of interacting galaxies in the constellation Corvus. Each galaxy's tidal force has drawn out a long tail of stars from the other. The Antennae are also known as NGC 4038 and NGC 4039.

Apollo Space Program: Successful U.S. lunar exploration program in which the Apollo spacecraft 1 to 6 were unmanned; 7 to 10 were manned but did not land; and 11, 12 and 14 to 17 landed and returned safely. The final Apollo flight (17) lasted from 7 to 19 December 1972, and left a considerable quantity of exploratory devices on the lunar surface.

Barred Spiral Galaxy: One whose center is elongated and spiral, or bar-shaped. A spiral galaxy whose nucleus is in the shape of a bar, at the ends of which the spiral arms start.

Barred Spiral Galaxy (NGC 1300): Located sixty-nine million light-years away, in the direction of the constellation Eridanus.

Big Bang Theory: This theory postulates that the universe began as a tiny but intense explosion almost fourteen billion years ago. An evolutionary model of cosmology in which the universe began in a state of extremely high density and temperature. According to this model, the universe has been expanding, thinning out, and cooling since its beginning.

Biomimicry: looking to nature for design inspiration, such as with photosynthesis, natural selection and self-sustaining ecosystems.

Black Hole: A massive region in space that is so dense within its radius that its gravitational field does not let anything escape from it, not even light. Scientists theorize that the average black hole is ten times larger than our Sun.

Bubble Nebula (NGC 7635): Ten light-years wide, it is located in the constellation Cassiopeia

Bug Nebula (NGC 6302): One of the brightest planetary nebulae known. The star inside has never been photographed, due to the gaseous surroundings. It is located about 4,000 light-years away in the constellation Scorpius.

Cassiopeia: Cassiopeia is an easily-seen constellation that is in the far northern sky. It circles the polestar (Polaris) throughout the year and also straddles the Milky Way.

Cat's Eye Nebula (NGC 6543): Considered one of the most complex planetary nebula yet discovered, the photos show intricate structures, and lots of evidence of gas in many forms. Cat's Eye is about 3,000 light years away from Earth.

Centaurus A Galaxy (NGC 1528): This provides one of the best views of an active supermassive black hole. It is the nearest known violent galaxy.

Chandra X-Ray Observatory: This is the world's most powerful X-ray telescope: it orbits around the Earth. It is a forty-five foot satellite that records X-rays from high-energy parts of the sky. It was launched on the Space Shuttle Columbia on July 23, 1999.

Cone Nebula (NGC 2264): A conical shaped conglomeration of gas and dust, it is twenty-five hundred light-years away.

Constellation: A group of stars, which, when viewed from Earth, seem to form some pattern.

Copernicus, Nicolaus (1473-1543): He was an amateur Polish astronomer who developed the revolutionary Copernican system, a model of the solar system in which all the planets orbit the Sun. His ideas overturned the old Ptolemaic System.

Crab Nebula (NGC 1952): The Crab Nebula (M1) is a cloud of intergalactic gas and dust. It is the remnant of a supernova that was seen on Earth in 1054. The Crab Nebula can be found in the constellation Taurus.

Cygnus: A constellation six hundred light-years from Earth. Cygnus (the swan) is shaped like a large cross. It is also known as the Northern Cross. It is seen along the Milky Way in the northern hemisphere.

Danger Zones: If star dust and gasses are too close to a new, hot star, they risk losing their star- and planet-making capability due to the radiation and winds generated by the new (or O) star.

Dark Energy: This nebulous form of matter makes up the vast bulk of deep space. It repels, rather than attracts, unlike gravity. Some astronomers see this as a wild card that may not be predicted.

Eagle Nebula (M16 NGC 6611): It consists of enormous columns of cool interstellar hydrogen gas and dust that are about 7,000 light-years from Earth, in the constellation Serpens.

Elephant's Trunk Nebula: In the constellation Cepheus, 2450 light-year from the Earth.

Eskimo Nebula (NGC 2392): It resembles a face in a parka. It is located about 5,000 light-years from Earth in the constellation Gemini. The Eskimo Nebula is a plantary nebula in Gemini. It is a dying sun-like star, whose outer layers have begun to drift off into space. It was first sighted by William Herschel in 1787.

Gagarin, Yuri (1934-1968): He became the first human to view earth from space. He was a Soviet cosmonaut and the first man to orbit the Earth. He piloted the Vostok 1 mission which launched April 12, 1961 and orbited the Earth. The flight lasted 108 minutes.

Galaxy: A galaxy is a huge group of stars and other celestial bodies bound together by gravitational forces. There are spiral, elliptical, and irregularly shaped galaxies. Our Sun and solar system are a small part of the Milky Way Galaxy.

Galilei, Galileo (1564-1642): An Italian mathematician, astronomer, and physicist. Galileo found that the speed at which bodies fall does not depend on their weight and did extensive experimentation with pendulums. In 1609, Galileo was the first person to use a telescope to observe the skies (after hearing about Hans Lippershey's newly-invented telescope).

Gamma-ray: Gamma rays are very high energy electromagnetic radiation, like light or X-rays, but much higher in energy and frequency (and shorter in wavelength).

Gamma Ray Burst: Mysterious and powerful astronomical phenomenon that emit short-lived flashes of gamma rays (extremely high-energy radiation). These bursts last only up to a few seconds, occur every day, and come from different parts of the sky.

Global Cluster (NGC 6397): This agglomeration of stars and dust and gas contains both red and white dwarf stars, among them the dimmest yet found, with a luminosity so faint that the light produced is similar to that of a birthday candle on Earth as seen from the Moon. This cluster is 8,500 light-years from our blessed planet.

Halo: This is a luminous ring that is sometimes seen surrounding the sun or the moon. Some parts of the halo are very bright, others are not very bright. The halo is produced as light is reflected and refracted through tiny, flat ice crystals in the atmosphere.

HD Number: The HD (Henry Draper) number is an identifying number assigned to the stars in the Henry Draper catalog. In this system, every star is classified by its stellar spectrum.

Heliocentrism: A concept whereby the sun is the center of our planetary system, with all the planets revolving around the Sun.

Helix Nebula (NGC 7293): This is a planetary nebula that has the largest angular diameter of any known planetary nebula. It is about 700 light-years or 140 parsecs away, in Aquarius. There is a dead star at the center of this nebula, providing an eerie glow that resembles an eye, with the dust surrounding it.

Henize 206: Located within the Large Magellanic Cloud in the Southern Hemisphere. It's considered an ideal cosmic laboratory that may resemble the distant universe in its chemical composition.

Hipparcos: The European Space Agency's satellite. It has claimed to have pinpointed more than 100 000 stars, 200 times more accurately than ever before.

Hubble, Edwin Powell (1889-1953): An American astronomer who was very influential in modern cosmology. He showed that other galaxies (besides the Milky Way) existed and observed that the universe is expanding (since the light from almost all other galaxies is red-shifted).

Hubble Space Telescope (or HST): A powerful telescope in orbit around the Earth. HST transmits pictures and spectra of objects in space without the interference of the atmosphere (which makes telescopic images from the ground have less detail). It was launched into space in April 1990 and was repaired in December, 1993. It was named for the American astronomer Edwin Hubble.

Infrared radiation: Infrared radiation is electromagnetic radiation that we can feel as heat.

Jupiter: The largest planet in our solar system, Jupiter has four larger and many smaller moons orbiting it. Scientists have discovered forty-nine so far. Its magnetic field is about twenty thousand times stronger than that of the Earth.

Kuiper, Gerard Peter (1905-1973): A Dutch-American astronomer who predicted the existence of the Kuiper belt in 1951. In 1948,

Kuiper Belt: A stable debris disc, filled with comets, in the Milky Way solar system. A region beyond Neptune in which at least 70,000 small objects (KBO's) orbit, including Quaoar and Sedna. This belt is located was discovered in 1992.

Lagoon Nebula: Situated five thousand light-years away in the constellation Sagittarius. Because of the unique environmental conditions, there are indications of tornadoes, resulting from the extreme differences in temperature.

Magellanic Clouds: Irregular-shaped galaxies, congregations of millions of stars. The irregular shape may be the result of a disturbance, perhaps a collision of two galaxies.

Mars: One of the closest planets which has fired man's imagination. It is termed the "red planet," the fourth planet from the sun.

Megaparsec (Mpc): A unit of distance that is equal to one million parsecs, 3.26×10^6 light-years or 3.085678×10^{19} kilometers. The Local Group of galaxies is roughly a megaparsec in diameter.

Milky Way Galaxy: A spiral galaxy—our sun and solar system are a small part of it. Most of the stars that we can see are in the Milky Way Galaxy. The main plane of the Milky Way looks like a faint band of white in the night sky. The Milky Way is about 100,000 light-years in diameter and 1,000 light-years thick.

Monoceros Light Echo (V8383): We find these spirals of dust 20,000 light-years from Earth. At one point it was 600,000 more luminous than out Sun, but then it faded away.

NASA: The National Aeronautics and Space Administration. It is the governmental agency that oversees space exploration for the USA.

National Oceanic and Atmospheric Administration's AVHRR sensor: the Advanced Very High Resolution Radiometer

Nebula: A huge, diffuse cloud of gas and dust in intergalactic space. The gas in nebulae (the plural of nebula) is mostly hydrogen gas (H_2).

Neutron Star: A very small, super-dense star which is composed mostly of tightly-packed neutrons. This hard-to-see body has a thin atmosphere of superhot hydrogen plasma and a crust. It has a diameter of about 5-10 miles (5-16 km) and a density of roughly 10 15 gm/cm3. Neutron stars are formed from supernova explosions. Also called a "magnestar."

Newton, Isaac (1642-1727): An English mathematician and physicist who invented calculus (simultaneously, but independently of Leibniz), formulated the laws of gravitation, investigated the nature of light. He discovered that sunlight is made of light of different colors. He also formulated the laws of motion. Newton also improved the design of the refracting telescope (using an objective mirror, instead of a lens), and it is now called a Newtonian telescope.

NGC (New General Catalog): A list of over 13,000 deep-sky celestial objects. It was developed in 1888 by John Dreyer. For example, the Great Nebula in Orion is NCG 1976 (and M42). NGC4414 (pictured above) is a spiral galaxy 60 million light-years away.

NGC 602: Small Magellanic Cloud

NGC 2440 Planetary Nebula: A white dwarf dwells at the centre of this nebula. It has a great deal of dust and gas and is located in the constellation Puppis, 4,000 light-years from Earth.

NGC 5194: A compact galaxy that has been passing behind the Whirlpool galaxy for hundreds of millions of years.

Nuclear Fission: A reaction in which an atom's nucleus is broken apart, releasing a tremendous amount of energy.

Nuclear Fusion: Nuclear fusion is an atomic reaction in which many nuclei (the centers of atoms) combine together to make a larger one (which is a different element). The result of this process is the release of a lot of energy (the resultant nucleus is smaller in mass than the sum of the ones that made it.

Omega Nebula, Swan Nebula (NGC 6618, M17): Located about 5,500 light-years from Earth, this is a hotbed of star formation.

Ophiuchus Constellation: (pronounced OFF-ee-YOOkuss), or "snake carrier," constellation about 375 light-years from Earth.

Orion: It is also known as "The Hunter," is a constellation. The brightest stars in Orion are Rigel. Betelgeuse, and Bellatrix. The Horsehead Nebula and the nebulae M42 and M43 (called the Orion nebula) are also in this constellation.

Orion Nebula (M42, NGC 1976): The Orion Nebula (M42 and M43) is a huge, nearby, turbulent gas cloud (mostly hydrogen) that is lit up by bright, young hot stars (including the asterism called Trapezium) that are developing within the nebula. This nebula is located about 1,500 light-years away from us towards the constellation of Orion.

O-star: Not a security feature on a new vehicle, this is a "scorching new star."

Parsec: Astronomical unit of distance, equal to 3.26 light-years.

Perseus constellation: Perseus is a constellation in the Milky Way in the Northern Hemisphere.

Photoevaporation: takes anywhere from 100,000 to about 1,000,000 years to create a new planet or star from swirling gas and dust.

Planck time: The first instant following the beginning of the expansion of the Universe, when the cosmic matter density was still so high that gravitational force acted as strongly as the other fundamental forces on the sub-atomic scale.

Planetary Nebulae: Glowing shrouds surrounding Sun-like stars. A planetary nebula is a nebula formed from by a shell of gas which was ejected from a certain kind of extremely hot star. As the giant star explodes, the core of the star is exposed.

Pleiades Star Cluster (M45): Also known as the Seven Sisters(and "Subaru" in Japan), though about one thousand stars actually make up the cluster. It is located in the constellation Taurus. It is estimated that it is about 440 light-years from Earth. It is the brightest open cluster of stars in the sky

Polycyclic Aromatic Hydrocarbons (PAH): comprised of carbon and hydrogen. The molecules are considered to be among the building blocks of life.

Proplyds: *See* **Protoplanetary Disks.**

Protoplanetary disks: Birth places of stars and planets. Also called "proplyds," they are the building blocks of solar systems. A protoplanetary disk is a rotating disk of dust that surrounds the central core of a developing solar system. This disk eventually coalesces into planets that orbit the star (which forms from the central core).

Proxima Centauri: Our Sun's closest star, nearly thirty trillion miles away.

Protostars: A protostar is a star that is still forming and nuclear fusion has not yet begun.

Quasars: A quasar (more recently known as a QSO, Quasi-Stellar Object) is a distant star-sized energy source in space with excess of ultraviolet.

RCW 49: Located 13,700 light-years away in a southern constellation, Centaurus. It has a reputation for being a fertile breeding ground for new stars, with more than twenty-two hundred in its "stellar nursery."

Reflection Nebula (NGC 1999): A nebula located in the constellation Orion. It is illuminated by a young star that is so hot, it is white in color. Much hotter and almost four time larger than our Sun.

Reflection Nebula (NGC 7129): Located 3,300 light-years from Earth in the constellation

Cepheus, it has approximately 130 young stars within its folds. A reflection nebula is a nebula that glows as the dust in it reflects the light of nearby stars.

Rho Oph Star-Forming Region: This region is about 407 light-years from Earth, relatively close. It contains more than 300 young stars who are a mere three hundred thousand years old.

Rosette Nebula: Found in the constellation Monoceros, this nebula looks like a rose bud, but those are super-hot stars, termed O-stars that are providing the light and heat.

Saturn: Galileo Galilei discovered this most distant planet with the aid of one of the first telescopes. It is composed mostly of hydrogen and helium, like Jupiter. It is 755 times larger than Earth.

Scorpius: Scorpius (the scorpion) is a constellation of the zodiac. This constellation is seen along the ecliptic between Libra and Sagittarius.

Small Magellanic Cloud (NGC 602): In the constellation Tucana it is about 200,000 light-years from the Earth. It is known as an older, dwarf galaxy, with many fewer stars than our galaxy.

Sombrero Galaxy (M104): The galaxy's hallmark is a brilliant white, bulbous core encircled by the thick dust lanes comprising the spiral structure of the galaxy. As seen from Earth, the galaxy is tilted nearly edge-on . . . This brilliant galaxy was named the Sombrero because of its resemblance to the broad rim and hightopped Mexican hat. [NASA]

Space Infrared Telescope Facility (SIRTF): an infrared cousin of the Hubble Space Telescope that followed Hubble into space in 2003. Spitzer detects infrared, longer wavelength light that our eyes cannot see. It detects the infrared energy, or heat, radiated by objects in space and is able to detect dust disks around stars.

Speed of Light: The speed at which electromagnetic waves can move in a vacuum = 186,000 miles per second. According to Einstein's theory of relativity, nothing can go faster than the speed of light.

Spiral Galaxy (M74,NGC 628): A "grand-design" spiral galaxy thirty-two million light-years away in the Pisces constellation. It is home to about a hundred billion stars, slightly fewer than those in our own Milky Way galaxy.

Spiral Galaxy NGC 3370: In the Constellation Leo. Spiral galaxies are galaxies with a central, dense area and spiraling arms. There are two types of spiral galaxies, "S" (normal spiral) and "SB" (barred spiral, with an elongated center).

Spirographic Nebula (IC 418): This planetary nebula lies some 2,000 light-years from Earth in the direction of the constellation Lepus.

Spitzer Space Telescope: The Spitzer Space Telescope (formerly SIRTF, the Space Infrared Telescope Facility) was launched into space by a Delta rocket from Cape Canaveral, Florida on 25 August 2003. During its mission, Spitzer will obtain images and spectra by detecting the infrared energy, or heat, radiated by objects in space between wavelengths of 3 and 180 microns (1 micron is one-millionth of a meter). Most of this infrared radiation is blocked by the Earth's atmosphere and cannot be observed from the ground

Standard Candles: Stars used to measure more distant, fainter stars. An object - usually a star or a galaxy of known intrinsic brightness. Measuring the apparent brightness of a standard candle yields its distance.

Star: Each star in the sky is a glowing ball of gas. Our sun is a medium-sized star. The first stars in the Universe appeared about 200 million years after the Big Bang (which occurred about 13.7 billon years).

Star Cluster: A group of stars positioned close together in space. A gravitationally bound aggregation of stars, smaller and less massive than galaxies. "Globular" clusters are the largest category; they are old, and may harbor hundreds of thousands to millions of stars, and are found both within and well away from the galactic disk.

Steady-State Theory: Some scientists believe that the universe always has been and always will be as it is. They say that the universe is not expanding and is uniform and infinite.

Sun: The center of our solar system, the Sun is the closest star to Earth, approximately ninety-four million miles from Earth. It is comprised mostly of ionized gas and is massive: 332,900 times larger than Earth.

Sunspot: Comparatively dark spot on the Sun's photosphere, commonly one of a (not always obvious) group of two. The center of a vast electrostatic field and a magnetic field of a single polarity (up to 4,000 gauss), a sunspot represents a comparatively cool depression (at a temperature of approximately 4,500 °C

Supergiant: A star that is much, much brighter and larger than our Sun. An extremely luminous star of large diameter and low density. A supergiant is the largest known type of star; some are almost as large as our entire solar system. Betelgeuse and Rigel are supergiants.

Supernova: A supernova is a huge explosion that occurs at the end of a mid- to heavyweight star's life. A supernova releases a tremendous amount of energy, expelling the outer layers of the star and becoming extremely bright. What remains is a neutron star or a black hole.

Telescope: A telescope is a device that makes faraway objects appear closer and larger, allowing us to see distant objects in space. The first refracting telescope was invented by Hans Lippershey in 1608.

Trapezium, The: The Trapezium is a star cluster located in the center of the Orion nebula.

UX Tau A: A young star that may only be a million years young

Veil Nebula: Contains the remains of a supernova that imploded aeons ago. It is 1,500 light-years from Earth.

VY Canis Majoris: A red supergiant star classified as a supergiant due to its massive luminosity. It is 5,000 light-years away and half a million times larger than our Sun.

W.M. Keck Telescope: The famed telescope atop Mauna Kea in Hawaii.

Whirlpool Galaxy (M51): is an interacting grand-design spiral galaxy located at a distance of approximately 23 million light-years in the constellation Canes Venatici.

CREDITS

The following abbreviations are for all images credited to the Hubble and Spitzer telescope as well as all the associated teams and institutions.

ACS - Advanced Camera for Surveys team
ASU - Arizona State University
AURA – Associated Universities for Research in Astronomy
COBE – Cosmic Background Explorer Satellite
CXC – Chandra X-Ray Center
ESO – European Southern Observatory
ESA - European Space Agency
DFSC – Goddard Spaceflight center
HHT – Hubble Heritage Team
HUDF – Hubble Ultra Deep Field
JPL - Jet Propulsion Laboratory
STScl – the Space Telescope Institute
SSC - Spitzer Science Center
UA - University of Arizona
UBC - University of British Columbia
UM – University of Minn.
UW – University of Wisconsin

Image Credits

Page 20 >NASA: 22 >NASA/JPL-Caltech: 24 >NASA/WMAP Science Team: 26 >NASA, ESA,HHT, (STScI/AURA) - ESA/Hubble Collaboration: 28 >NASA, HHT, (STScI/AURA): 30 > NASA/JPL-Caltech/R. Hurt (SSC): 32 >NASA, ESA, S. Beckwith (STScI) HUDF Team: 34 >NASA, HHT, (STScI/AURA): 36 >J.P. Harrington, K.J. Borkowski (Univ of MD), and NASA 38 >NASA/JPL-Caltech/K. Su (Univ. of Ariz.): 40 >NASA/JPL-Caltech/N. Flagey (IAS/SSC) & A. Noriega-Crespo (SSC/Caltech): 42 > NASA,HHT, (STScI/AURA): 44 > NASA and Adolf Schaller (for STScI): 46 > NASA/CXC/ M.Weiss:

48 > NASA/CXC/M.Weiss: 50 > Robert Gendler 54 > NASA/JPL-Caltech/T. Pyle (SSC): 56 > NASA/JPL-Caltech/T. Pyle (SSC): 58 > NASA/JPL-Caltech/T. Pyle (SSC): 60 > NASA/JPL-Caltech/R. Hurt (SSC): 62 > NASA/JPL-Caltech/R. Hurt: 64, 66, 68, 70 > NASA/JPL-Caltech/T. Pyle (SSC): 72, 74 > NASA 76 > Don Davis, NASA: 78 > NASA: 82, 84 > Quills Design: 92 > X-ray: NASA/CXC/J.Hester (ASU); Optical: NASA/ESA/J.Hester & A.Loll (ASU); Infrared: NASA/JPL-Caltech/R.Gehrz (Univ. Minn.): 94 >NASA, HHT and A. Riess (STScI): 96 > NASA/JPL-Caltech/E. Churchwell (UW): 98 > NASA, ESA, S. Beckwith, HHT, (STScI/AURA): 100 > NASA, A. Fruchter and the ERO Team (STScI): 102 > NASA, HHT, (STScI /AURA): 104 > NASA/JPL-Caltech/W. Reach (SSC/Caltech): 106 > NASA, ESA, M. Robberto (STS/ESA), Hubble Space Telescope Orion Treasury Project Team: 108 > NASA, ESA, and B. Whitmore (STScI): 110 > NASA, ESA, HHT, (STScI/AURA)- ESA/Hubble Collaboration: 112 > NASA, ESA, HHT, (STScI/AURA): 114 > NASA, ESA and AURA/Caltech: 116 > NASA/JPL-Caltech/T. Megeath (Harvard-Smithsonian CfA): 118 > NASA: 120 > NASA, HHT, (STScI/AURA): 122 > NASA, ESA, M. Robberto (Space Telescope Science Institute/ESA), Hubble Space Telescope Orion Treasury Project Team: 124 > NASA, ESA, HHT, (STScI/AURA) - ESA/Hubble Collaboration: 126 > J.P. Harrington and

K.J. Borkowski (University of Maryland),
NASA: 128 > NASA, HHT,
(STScI/AURA):
130 >John Bahcall (Institute for Advanced
Study, Princeton), Mike Disney
(University of Wales), NASA: 132 >
NASA/JPL-Caltech/Z. Balog, (UA/Univ.
of Szeged): 134 > NASA: 136 > NASA,
H. Ford (JHU), G. Illingworth
(USCS/LO), M. Clampin (STScI), G.
Hartig (STScI), ACS Science Team: 138
> A. Caulet (ST-ECF, ESA), NASA:
140 > NASA: 142 > NASA: 144 > NASA:
146 > C.R. O'Dell (Rice University),
NASA: 148 > NASA, NOAO, ESA, the
Hubble Helix Nebula Team, M. Meixner
(STScI), and T.A. Rector (NRAO):
150 > NASA, ESA and J. Hester (ASU):
152 > NASA, ESA, HHT,
(STScI/AURA)-ESA/Hubble
Collaboration: 154 > NASA, J. Hester
and P. Scowen (ASU): 156 >
NASA/CXC/ASU/JHST/ Hester et al:
158 > NASA, ESA and A.Zijlstra
(UMIST, Manchester, UK: 160 > NASA,
HHT (STScI/AURA)-ESA/Hubble
Collaboration: 162 > NASA, HHT
(STScI/AURA): 164 > NASA, ESA, and
H. Richer (UBC):
166 > NASA / JPL-Caltech / O. Krause
(Steward Observatory):
168 > NASA/JPL-Caltech/L. Allen
(Harvard-Smithsonian Center for
Astrophysics): 170 > NASA and A. Riess
(STScI): 172 > NASA/HHT/
(STScI/AURA): 174 >
NASA/HHT/(STScI/AURA): 176 >
NASA:
178 >NASA and E. Karkoschka (UA): 180
> NASA, ESA, HHT, (STScI/AURA)-
ESA/Hubble Collaboration: 182 >
NASA/JPL-Caltech/K. Su (UA): 184 >
NASA/CXC/CfA/R.Kraft et al: 186 >
NASA, ESA, HHT, (STScI/AURA): 188
> Bruce Balick (UW), Vincent Icke
(Leiden University, The Netherlands),
Garrelt Mellema (Stockholm University),
and NASA: 190 > NASA, HHT,
(STScI/AURA): 192 > NASA, HHT,

(STScI/AURA): 194 > NASA, ESA, S.
Beckwith (STScI) and the HUDF Team:

NASA News Releases

44> http://hubblesite.org/newcenter/
archive/releases
/2002/10/image/h/ 55 > http://www.
spitzer.caltech.edu/Media
/releases/ssc2005-15/release.shtml
57 > http://www.spitzer.caltech.edu/Media/
releases/ssc2007-16/release.shtml 59 >
http://www.spitzer.caltech.edu/
Media/releases/ssc2007-14/release.shtml
61 > http://gallery.spitzer.caltech.edu/
Imagegallery/
image.php?image_name=ssc2004-20b
63 > http://gallery.spitzer.caltech.edu/
Imagegallery/image.
php?image_name=ssc2007-14d
65 > http://www.spitzer.caltech.edu/Media/
releases/ssc2005-26/release.shtml
67 > http://gallery.spitzer.caltech.edu/Image
gallery/
image.php?image_name=ssc2007-08c
69 > http://www.spitzer.caltech.edu/
Media/happenings/
20071128/index.shtml
71 > http://www.spitzer.caltech.edu/Media
/releases/ssc2004-22/release.shtml
73 > http://oceancolor.gsfc.nasa.gov/Sea
WiFS/HTML/SeaWiFS.
BiosphereAnimation.html
93 > http://gallery.spitzer.caltech.edu/
Imagegallery/ image.php?image_name
=sig06-028
95 > http://hubblesite.org/newcenter/
archive/ releases/2003/24/image/a
97 > http://www.spitzer.caltech.edu/Media
/releases/ssc2004-08/ssc2004-08a.shtml
99 > http://hubblesite.org/newcenter/
archive/ releases/2005/12/image/a
101 > http://hubblesite.org/newcenter
/archive/ releases/2000/07/image/a
103 > http://hubblesite.org/newcenter
/archive/ releases/1998/28/image/e
105 > http://www.spitzer.caltech.edu/Media
/releases/ssc2003-06/ssc2003-06b.shtml
107 > http://hubblesite.org/newcenter/
archive/ releases/2006/01/image/a/

109 > http://hubblesite.org/newscenter/ archive/ releases/2006/46/image/a

111 > http://hubblesite.org/newscenter/ archive/ releases/2007/30/image/a

113 > http://hubblesite.org/newscenter/ archive/ releases/2005/01/image/a

115 > http://hubblesite.org/newscenter/ archive/ releases/2004/20/image/a/

117 > http://www.spitzer.caltech.edu/ Media/releases/ssc2004-02/release.shtml

121 > http://hubblesite.org/newscenter/ archive/ releases/2000/10/image/a

123 > http://hubblesite.org/newscenter/ archive/ releases/2006/01/image/q

125 > http://hubblesite.org/newscenter/ archive/ releases/2007/04/image/a

127 > http://hubblesite.org/newscenter/ archive/ releases/1995/01/image/a

129 > http://hubblesite.org/newscenter/ archive/ releases/2004/04/image/a

131 > http://hubblesite.org/newscenter/ archive/ releases/1996/35/image/a

133 > http://www.spitzer.caltech.edu/Media /releases/ssc2007-08/ssc2007-08b.shtml

137 > http://hubblesite.org/newscenter/ archive/ releases/2002/11/image/b

139 > http://hubblesite.org/newscenter/ archive/ releases/1996/38/image/b

147 > http://hubblesite.org/newscenter/ archive/ releases/1992/29/text/

149 > http://hubblesite.org/newscenter/ archive/ releases/2003/11/image/b

151 > http://hubblesite.org/newscenter/ archive/ releases/2003/13/image/a

153 > http://hubblesite.org/newscenter/ archive/ releases/2007/03/full/

155 > http://hubblesite.org/newscenter/ archive/ releases/1995/44/image/b

157 > http://hubblesite.org/newscenter/ archive/ releases/2002/24/text/

159 > http://hubblesite.org/newscenter/ archive/ releases/2004/46/image/a

161 > http://hubblesite.org/newscenter/ archive/ releases/2007/41/image/a

163 > http://hubblesite.org/newscenter/ archive/ releases/2003/28/image/a

165 http://hubblesite.org/newscenter/ archive/ releases/2006/37/image/a

167 > http://www.spitzer.caltech.edu/ Media/releases/ssc2005-14/release.shtml

169 > http://www.spitzer.caltech.edu/ Media/releases/ssc2008-03/release.shtml

171 > http://hubblesite.org/newscenter/ archive/releases/star/ 2004/12/results/50/ layout/%202/

173 > http://hubblesite.org/newscenter /archive/releases/ 2001/23/image/a/

175 > http://hubblesite.org/newscenter/ archive/releases/ 2004/10/image/a

177 > http://solarsystem.nasa.gov/planets /profile.cfm? Object=Jupiter

181 > http://hubblesite.org/newscenter /archive/releases/ 2008/16/image/a/

183 > http://www.spitzer.caltech.edu/ Media/releases/ssc2007-03/release.shtml

185 > http://chandra.harvard.edu/photo /2008/cena/

187 > http://hubblesite.org/newscenter/ archive/releases/ 2001/05/image/a/

189 > http://hubblesite.org/newscenter/ archive/releases/ 1997/38/image/a/

191 > http://hubblesite.org/newscenter/ archive/releases/ 2000/28/image/a

193 > http://hubblesite.org/newscenter/ archive/releases/ 2002/05/image/a

195 > http://hubblesite.org/newscenter /archive/releases/ 2004/07/image/a/

Websites to visit for additional information:

http://TheSecretDoorway.com
http://hubblesite.org/
http://www.spitzer.caltech.edu/
http://www.jpl.nasa.gov/
http://www.nasa.gov/
http://www.jwst.nasa.gov/
http://www.worldwidetelescope.org/
http://chandra.harvard.edu/
http://oceancolor.gsfc.nasa.gov/SeaWiFS/ HTML/SeaWiFS.BiosphereAnimation. html

Scriptural Quote: Isaiah 40: 25, 26: New Living Translation

INDEX